IF I'D ONLY **KNOWN** THAT

Common Mistakes in Equity Compensation and What to Do About Them

IF I'D ONLY **KNOWN** THAT

Common Mistakes in Equity Compensation and What to Do About Them

EDITOR AND COAUTHOR

Achaessa James

CONTRIBUTORS

Bruce Brumberg, Jon F. Doyle, Kate Forsyth, Jennifer George, Steve Kifer, Kim Kovacs, Paul Leisey, Takis Makridis, Mark Miller, David Outlaw, Corey Rosen, Robyn Shutak, Jim Sillery, Mike Stevens, Dan Walter, Fred Whittlesey, and Yan Zhao

The National Center for Employee Ownership
Oakland, California

This publication is designed to provide accurate and authoritative information in regard to the subject matter covered. It is sold with the understanding that the publisher is not engaged in rendering legal, accounting, or other professional service. If legal advice or other expert assistance is required, the services of a competent professional person should be sought.

Legal, accounting, and other rules affecting business often change. Before making decisions based on the information you find here or in any publication from any publisher, you should ascertain what changes might have occurred and what changes might be forthcoming. The NCEO's Web site (including the members-only area) and newsletter for members provide regular updates on these changes. If you have any questions or concerns about a particular issue, check with your professional advisor or, if you are an NCEO member, call or email us.

If I'd Only Known That
Achaessa James, editor and coauthor
Copyedited by Deborah Willoughby and Pam Chernoff
Book design by Scott S. Rodrick

The National Center for Employee Ownership
1736 Franklin Street, 8th Floor
Oakland, CA 94612
(510) 208-1300
(510) 272-9510 (fax)
Web site: www.nceo.org

ISBN-10: 1-932924-81-7
ISBN-13: 978-1-932924-81-7

Contents

Not Knowing...and Not Knowing You Don't Know

Achaessa James, NCEO

I started administering equity compensation plans in 1999. I'd been a paralegal for many years and was burned out from an intense area of practice. I thought I'd switch to something less stressful, so I took a position with a boutique firm that specialized in working with startup and early-stage companies. We focused on corporate formation, venture capital financing, and corporate transactions like mergers, acquisitions, and IPOs. We did a few all-nighters at the legal printers, but there were no life-or-death issues at stake, and I was satisfied that I'd made a good career move.

Part of the job was issuing stock certificates for the investment transactions. And, while we were at it, we also kept track of the stock options and restricted stock the companies issued to their employees and executives. On a spreadsheet. The thought still makes me shudder.

Coming into this new practice area, I took it upon myself to learn the depth and breadth of corporate governance nuances in issuing stock and options, and Securities and Exchange Commission (SEC) regulations for filing registration statements, but I had no idea at the time that tax-qualified options could only be granted to employees after they actually started working for the company. I had no idea that those same incentive stock options (ISOs) only had 90 days to be exercised after an employee terminated. And, worst of all, I had no idea that a pattern of noncompliance with those rules could disqualify an entire plan! Those were tax issues, not legal issues. And thank goodness mandatory equity compensation expensing wasn't in place back then!

I'm confident that my supervising attorneys knew the tax rules and made sure that ISO grants were properly issued to active employees, but I could have been much more valuable to them if I had known firsthand about those regulations. Indeed, I knew that there had to be more to it than keeping a spreadsheet, so I started becoming active in equity compensation professional groups and found out about the Certified Equity Professional (CEP) designation offered by the Certified Equity Professional Institute at Santa Clara University. But the dot-com bubble was just starting to leak and my firm didn't want to make that investment, and I soon moved over to work on the venture capital side of the fence.

Working with private equity investors gave me a deeper insight into equity issuances of hundreds of portfolio companies. I was confronted with evidence every day that administering equity compensation plans was done only haphazardly, as a side job, ancillary to the more important job of issuing stock for investments. I did corporate governance audits on dozens of portfolio companies, and an inordinate number of equity compensation awards on those companies' cap tables did not match the corresponding board authorizations in one aspect or another.

It wasn't until I started consulting as an educator on corporate governance that I realized that many in-house attorneys for startup companies had come from non-corporate backgrounds. One attorney at a well-known dot-com had come from a highly respected international healthcare nonprofit but knew nothing about corporate governance and how corporate capitalization was created. And he knew even less about issuing tax-qualified ISOs, even though he was responsible for guiding the board of directors in making those issuances in compliance with Internal Revenue Service (IRS) regulations. Thank goodness he'd decided to sit in on the training I gave to his new in-house stock plan administrator!

Then, in late 2006, I returned to active plan administration for an outsource accounting firm, just in time to usher in mandatory equity compensation expensing under FAS 123(R)—and I knew without a doubt that there was so much I didn't know that I didn't even know what questions to ask. I immediately called the CEP Institute to sign up for the next exam and paid for my own books and tuition because it was that important.

I tell this story not as the confessional that it feels like but to give weight to the fact that there is no single clear career path to becoming an equity compensation professional. I and many of my peers started as a paralegal. Many others come from accounting firms; others from human resources; others from executive compensation consulting firms; others from administration software vendors. And each of us brings our own perspective and our own focus on the rules that apply to our foundational profession—law, tax, accounting, benefits, plan design—which leaves a lot of room for issues outside of our professional expertise to fall through the cracks. And that is precisely why I am thankful every day for the CEP Institute and the National Center for Employee Ownership (NCEO). The CEP program is the only program that brings all of the elements of the equity compensation industry together in a comprehensive curriculum. When I was studying for my CEP certification exams and afterward, before I came to work here, I relied heavily on the NCEO as a resource for continuing education, for industry updates, and for getting answers from subject matter experts on tricky industry questions.

It may well be that the equity compensation industry is among the most highly regulated industries. Building and using a professional network is probably the most efficient and cost-effective way an equity compensation professional can keep abreast of our ever-changing industry. This book contains some humorous and painful examples of what happens when otherwise competent and responsible professionals don't know what they don't know and fail to use their professional networks before taking actions that result in consequences that range from the merely awkward to the downright serious.

And now I'm going to use my professional network and repurpose a bit of the introduction to the NCEO's counterpart book for ESOPs called "Don't Do That!" that was published in 2010. Corey Rosen, the NCEO executive director and editor of that book, said it so well, there's no point in my recreating the wheel:

The "don't do that's" range from seemingly mundane operational issues to more clearly explosive issues.

Donald Rumsfeld famously said of the Iraq war that "There are known knowns. These are things we know that we know. There are known unknowns. That is to say, there are things that we know we don't know. But there are also unknown unknowns—the ones we don't know we don't know." He got a lot of flack for that, but what he said makes a lot of sense. He should have added one more, however—the unknown knowns, the things we think we know that we really don't. As Satchel Paige put it, "It's not what you don't know that hurts you, it's what you know that just ain't so." This book is mostly about the unknown knowns and the ain't so's—people thinking they could or should do something they couldn't or shouldn't.

This book is not a comprehensive compendium of all the things you shouldn't do. That list could go on and on. But it does try to cover the most common kinds of problems that occur. To do that, I asked several of the leading equity compensation lawyers, plan administrators, tax and accounting consultants, and software vendors to contribute cases and lessons. Many have generously done so. The rest of the cases and lessons are drawn either from conversations I have had with companies over the years or from litigation. A special thanks to MyStockOptions.com founder Bruce Brumberg, who gave me access to the site's extensive FAQ and Ask the Expert column that provided significant fodder for this book.

The book presents brief case histories, each followed by the lessons on what should have been done. Unless the case comes from litigation, which means the names of the companies and other players are already public, the identities of the companies are well disguised. In a few instances, the cases are amalgamations of a few companies' experiences that together form a more illustrative picture. Some of the material overlaps because similar issues come up in different areas. But we assume you may not read this all in one sitting, so we made the discussions more freestanding.

A few key themes emerge in this book:

- *Make sure your advisors really know what they are doing.* Your advisors should be able to show you a client list you can call for referrals, demonstrate involvement in equity compensation organizations (they should at least be members and preferably speak at meetings or write articles), and have the required professional certifications for their fields.
- *Get educated yourself.* Qualified as your advisors may be, they are still human and can make mistakes. More commonly, they have particular approaches to equity compensation that may not fit your

needs as well as other approaches do. Unless you know what the alternatives are for such things as award policies, valuation, vesting, etc., you are limited by their preferred ways of doing things.

- *Don't be overconfident about what you know.* Socrates said, "The only true wisdom is in knowing you know nothing." He might have been unable to make any decisions as a corporate executive with an attitude that cautious. But it is wise to be wary. Ask a lot of questions, especially: "Is there any other way we could do this that might work better?" and "If we do this, whose interests are we really protecting—the participants' or those of someone else?"

The intention of this book is not to leave you so shaken by nightmares of dire possibilities that you wish you had never heard of equity compensation. The truth is that equity compensation is a widely used and powerful tool for attracting and retaining top employees in a competitive marketplace, and that will not change anytime soon. If you keep up with the things not to do and learn about the best practices through our Webinars, books, meetings, and calling us, chances are very good that you will find an equity compensation strategy that works for your company.

Fixing the Problems

If, after reading one or more of these pieces, you realize you have a problem that might get you in trouble with the IRS or SEC, step one is to retain qualified counsel. Don't hope that you can quietly fix the problem and the agencies won't notice. If you get audited and the IRS finds the problem, you could be facing serious penalties, and sometimes your employees can face penalties, too. If your equity compensation plan or stock valuation is out of line with SEC guidelines, it can interfere with an acquisition or IPO and be costly to remedy. If it's too late for an ounce of prevention, the pound of cure is still less expensive than a house call.

A Note on Contributors

This book is a collaborative effort. We asked NCEO members to contribute their favorite "If I'd Only Known That" cases, and many responded.

The rest of the book was written by NCEO staff. A more detailed biography of the contributors is at the end of the book.

The Specifics in Brief

Whether the problems were related to tax, law, accounting, performance awards, executive compensation, corporate governance, international issues, corporate transactions, consultants, valuation, or culture, they all had their roots in the following three categories:

Communication and Education

A large majority of these stories can be traced directly back to the failure to communicate between company stakeholders, the failure to communicate understandably to employees, failure to properly educate employees, and the administrator's lack of a specialized education in equity compensation issues. Here are some of the problems that arose when communication or education were deficient:

- Executives negotiating a corporate transaction didn't think that equity compensation would have an impact on the deal so they didn't do proper due diligence. In one particular case, the equity compensation turned out to be a deal breaker; in a couple of others, it cost the company hundreds of thousands of dollars in penalties and interest to bring the company into tax law compliance.
- Failure of the plan administrator to communicate with the payroll department resulted in a missed employee stock purchase plan (ESPP) payroll contribution and forced the company to manually process hundreds of catch-up contributions; missing the payroll deposit for withholding on a restricted stock unit (RSU) payout in excess of $100,000 incurred thousands of dollars in penalties and interest for the late deposit.
- Failure of a plan administrator to properly manage the tracking of tax-qualified stock resulted in an IRS audit, big penalties and interest, and 13 years of remedial activities.
- And most avoidable of all, failure to have a proper employee education program consistently resulted in the employees un-

dervaluing or placing a zero value on the awards themselves. If the employees aren't provided enough information so that they understand the value of the award, what's the point of making the awards?

Plan Design and Modifications

The second most common problem area was poor plan design and failure to consider the long-term consequences of modifications. Here are some of the problems that arose when design or modifications were not well thought out:

- The repurposing of a benefit agreement for use in equity compensation ended up in one company paying ongoing annual cash bonuses to terminated employees years after termination.
- Small broad-based RSU awards ended up costing the employees about $200 in tax preparation fees over two years to account for less than $100 in net gain over the same period.
- A bad phantom stock design cost the company an IPO and resulted, instead, in a steeply discounted sale.
- A U.S. company's decision to process the currency conversion for a foreign subsidiary's ESPP participation only once per year resulted in all of the foreign employees losing 100% of the value of their payroll contributions.
- Failure to check the math for potential outcomes before implementing the plan resulted in costly cash payout obligations for a phantom stock plan.
- Multiple instances of companies using cookie-cutter plans from compensation consultants ran contrary to long-term business goals or industry standards and ended up costing the companies in both money and employee satisfaction.
- Modifications to existing plans placed awards issued from the new plan and the old plan in conflict and resulted in employee dissatisfaction and costly "make whole" activities to close corporate transactions.

Administration, Policy, and Process

A close third, problems with administration, policy, and process were the stickiest in terms of who takes front line responsibility, how to ultimately make sure that the company stays compliant with all of the laws, regulations, and standards that govern the equity compensation awards, and how to make sure that employees have all the tools they need to make the most of their equity awards. It's easy to see, however, that the roots of these problems really lie with having an administrator who is not properly educated in equity compensation issues. Here are some highlights of stories in this category:

- Failure of the plan administrator to have a communication policy in place with regard to post-termination exercise periods, 83(b) elections, alternative minimum tax (AMT) implications of ISO exercises, etc., ended up costing the affected employees significant sums of money.
- Failure to have an approval policy in place to obtain Web-based stock prices resulted in using an erroneous closing stock price for processing an ESPP purchase and had to be backed out months later along with all of the interim sale and transfer transactions.
- Failure to have a process in place for integrating software updates ended up costing hundreds of staff hours in one case and delayed the processing of an ESPP purchase for several days in another.
- Failure to have a policy in place for managing multiple active plans with conflicting terms resulted in the issuance of new options on the old plan to use up forfeit option shares in the reserve pool, ultimately creating an administration nightmare for current-year grants and jeopardizing a corporate transaction, making the acquiring company very unhappy.

We hope you enjoy this compilation. With 63 stories from some of the equity compensation industry's most qualified experts, we're sure you'll find at least one that sounds familiar, one that makes you laugh out loud, and one that scares you enough to look at your own equity compensation activities more closely.

Chapter 1

Plan Design and Modifications

It all starts here. If you have a good plan design, then you nip in the bud many of the problems that arose in the stories in this chapter. What does a good plan design look like? To start with, it depends upon your company, your industry, and what you want to accomplish by giving equity compensation. Once those bases are covered, the plan needs to incorporate terms and conditions and administrative mechanisms that make the plan efficient to administer and that make sense for your company's situation.

Certainly there are thousands of templates floating around in attorney offices, equity compensation consulting offices, and even on the Internet. But adoption of one of those templates without customizing it to your company's specific goals is just asking for trouble. On the other hand, several of these stories also demonstrate how over-customizing a plan, or adapting a different type of plan, can create administrative headaches and award recipient dissatisfaction and end up costing the company a lot of money. Customization is a fine balance. As demonstrated in *You're So Special,* sometimes an equity award isn't even the right vehicle for what you want to accomplish. The point here is to put real thought into what you want to achieve with the awards, and with that in mind it will be fairly clear what plan design will work best for you.

Modifying an equity compensation plan also requires forethought. In fact, in all the modification stories in this chapter the common cause of what went wrong was lack of forethought. The failure to make an in-depth analysis of the long-term consequences of the proposed change can be exceedingly costly. Again, don't just take some consultant's word for it. Do your own math. Do your own stress test and include a best case, neutral, and worst case scenario. Look at it from an award recipient's perspective, from an auditor's perspective, from the IRS's perspective.

The most important advice here is twofold: Don't rush, and think it through before implementation.

What Do You Mean by "Revenue"?

Fred Whittlesey, Hay Group

A company implemented a long-term performance share plan with two performance measures: revenue and operating profit. The plan did not include a specific definition of either measure; instead, it referenced generally accepted accounting principles (GAAP) for the definitions of both revenue and operating profit. Historically, however, the company had tracked revenue for purposes of its various annual executive and sales incentive plans differently from GAAP. As revenue recognition rules changed for the industry, the finance group adjusted its accounting procedures but never thought to mention the changes to the plan administrator or the grant recipients.

At the end of the three-year period, the executive participants were ecstatic. According to their historic revenue tracking methods, they had not only exceeded the operating profit target but had hit the maximum on the revenue measure—with those numbers, they were in line for a 160% payout. Then came the bad news from the finance group—using the updated GAAP definitions as directed in the plan, the revenue component was actually below the threshold for the plan, and the plan design called for performance on both measures being at threshold or better for any plan payout. The executives were not happy when the payout number unexpectedly became zero.

Lessons

Regulations governing equity compensation are constantly changing. An unexpected change like this could happen on almost any front, from accounting, to taxes, to securities laws—making what seemed like a good idea suddenly not so good. Here are some useful policies to incorporate into plan administration to avoid surprises:

- Clearly specify the definitions of performance measures in the plan documents.

- Anticipate changes in accounting rules that could occur over the course of the plan.
- Cultivate strong relationships with tax, finance, legal, and human resources, preferably holding an annual stakeholders meeting, to keep informed of regulatory and business changes that may affect equity compensation plans and outstanding grants.
- Be active in industry professional groups to stay on top of how regulatory changes affect your company's plans.

The imminent shift to international financial reporting standards (IFRS) in the U.S. will present many such challenges. Three-year grants made as early as 2012 will be affected if IFRS adoption occurs in 2014.

Take My Equity, Please—The Retention Program That Forgot to Retain

Fred Whittlesey, Hay Group

A publicly traded financial services firm used common forms of long-term equity-based compensation but was influenced by its close business relationships with the venture capital and private equity sectors and desired to emulate that form of equity participation. Thus each year the company granted key employees the equivalent of "carried interest" in various investment funds, an unusual form of equity allowing them to participate in gains and distributions resulting from the company's investment activities. The "equity participation" distributions were made in cash and, due to indirect participation, were simply cash distributions (bonuses) to the participating employees from the company. They were not eligible for the capital gains treatment of similar awards in investment firms. The equity participation grants had 10-year terms—meaning that once the grant was made, the employee was entitled to distributions for the next 10 years.

Years later, a consultant was hired to include these equity participation awards in an employee total compensation analysis. The company complained that the program was too expensive to continue, yet there were very few current employees who had active equity participation grants.

In reviewing the plan document, the consultant discovered that the company had included one provision that is somewhat common in the investment firm world but didn't make much sense in the company's situation: award recipients were entitled to retain their awards and receive the distributions even if they terminated employment with the company, regardless of the reason for termination. As a result, an employee could be a star performer one year, receive an equity participation award, commit an egregious act the next year, be fired, and continue to receive compensation from that award for nine more years.

The equity participation award plan was indeed too expensive, paying all of those former employees.

Lessons

This is a good example of repurposing a document designed for a different use and failing to have an equity compensation professional vet the results and analyze the potential consequences before putting the plan into place. What works in one field might not work in another. When designing a plan, have a generous dose of respect for the law of unintended consequences and consider the repercussions of unusual situations. If you want terminated employees to be eligible for awards going forward, do you really want that apply to all kinds of terminations? If the awards are equity-based, do you understand *all* of the tax consequences of guaranteed vesting?

In addition, consider how big a financial burden guaranteed awards could put on the company over time—not just using the most likely scenarios, but also considering the effects of huge spikes or drops in the company's stock price. Once you've made a 10-year promise, you'll be stuck with it, so do your homework

When Equity Compensation Is a Negative Number

Fred Whittlesey, Hay Group

A company with a strong egalitarian ownership philosophy provided stock option grants to every employee, even part-time store workers—a highly unusual practice in the industry. The minimum option grant size was 50 options subject to the company's standard vesting schedule: 25% annually for four years (despite the resulting rounding problems).

When the company decided to move to restricted stock unit (RSU) grants to deal with dilution and stock price volatility issues, it began granting 12 RSUs (reflecting a 4:1 conversion ratio from options, rounded down) to the nonexempt employees with the same four-year vesting schedule. The company's stock price continued to decline due to changes in the industry and economic weakness.

When the first tranche of three RSUs vested a year later, at $14 each, these employees vested in $42 worth of RSUs. After withholding they netted less than $30 for the year's vested shares. It seemed like a joke, and the employees laughed about their newfound riches, until the following year when the affected employees began their annual tax reporting preparations.

Rather than simply withhold shares from the affected employees' paychecks or have them write small checks to the company for the taxes due on the $42 gain, the company had simply reduced the number of shares issued to the employees, which resulted in a "sale" of the withheld shares to the company. Unfortunately, the small short-term capital gain stemming from the difference between the price at the vest event and the price when shares were sold to cover tax withholding eliminated the employees' ability to use the Form 1040EZ when they filed their income taxes. That meant that the affected employees had to instead file full Form 1040s, with many of them requiring the assistance of a tax preparer—which cost far more than the $30 they realized from the shares.

To rescue this situation, the company then accelerated vesting on the three remaining tranches of RSUs, delivering another $108 in value—and one final year of tax impact for the plan participants.

In the end, each employee ended up paying an average of $200 in tax preparer fees for a net gain of less than $100.

Lessons

I've always wanted a good excuse to quote this Scottish poem in its entirety. Here is the English translation:

> The best laid schemes of Mice and Men
> oft go awry,
> And leave us nothing but grief and pain,
> For promised joy!
> —Robert Burns, "To a Mouse" (November 1785)

Even assuming that a qualified equity compensation professional was involved in the decision to move from option grants to RSUs, the plan went off track because no one bothered to do the math. The key, really, is setting all good intentions aside and taking a specific look at what is planned and what the possible results could be. I recently attended an equity compensation conference session where one of the panelists recommended a three-prong analysis: the good, the neutral, and the ugly...uh, bad. If that had been done before the board authorized the 4:1 RSU exchange, this frustrating situation would have been brought to light and the company could have structured a reward program for its nonexempt employees that didn't cost the employees more than they received in the bargain.

Take note:

- When doing conversions and substitutions, always remember to run some sample math scenarios on the largest resulting award, the average award, and the smallest award using a rise/neutral/fall stock price. Sometimes it just makes sense to structure the awards differently for different groups of recipients.
- Remember to take vesting tranches into account when looking at the possible gain treatment of an award; the award recipient rarely receives the benefit of the entire award at one time, and if the incremental amounts are small enough they can result in a cost to the award recipient and not the motivation and retention that the award was designed to inspire.
- When award numbers get down into the double digits and vesting tranches get down into the single digits, the stock price really has to be in the triple digits before the net gain will be sufficient to justify the increased administrative burden for employee tax returns.

Mega-Grant to CEO

Fred Whittlesey, Hay Group

A new CEO signed a three-year employment agreement when he joined the company. When his first three-year term expired, he began negotiating a new three-year contract. He also wanted three years of grants in the first year to renew his employment agreement—essentially a new-hire grant for his "rehire."

As a compromise, the company's executive compensation consultant suggested adjusting vesting so that the same number of shares vested as if they were granted over three years (11-22-33-22-11). In addition, the compensation committee granted the options at a premium price, 25% above fair market value on the date of grant, with the thought that the premium price and the vesting schedule created a more shareholder-friendly mega-grant. The compensation committee emphasized in that year's proxy statement that the CEO would receive no additional grants in the next three years due to this front-loaded grant.

This was just before the financial crisis.

Six months later, the stock price was down by 50% due primarily to the Great Recession, and the next year the CEO pointed to his underwater options with a "what are you going to do for me now?" attitude. The compensation committee ultimately relented and made an additional "retention" grant to the CEO, resulting both in four years worth of options granted in less than a two-year period and displeased shareholders.

Lessons

This situation highlights the risk of pursuing front-loaded stock option grants. Front-loaded grants are effective in a rising market—when stock price volatility and economic uncertainty are dominating factors. However, when the market takes a downturn, front-loaded grants, especially those with premium pricing, quickly become a burden instead of an incentive. An executive too quick to ask for an adjustment often ends up looking greedy to the shareholders and creating bad blood with the board, neither of which is good for bringing a company through a difficult time or for obtaining shareholder approval of future compensation.

The Best Intentions, the Worst Invention

Dan Walter, Performensation Consulting

A company came to the outsourcing provider I was working for with a plan of its own invention. Rather than implement a standard employee stock purchase plan (ESPP), the company had designed its own plan that looked like an ESPP. Participants were allowed payroll deductions during a 12-month contribution period and at the end of the year received in return a cash payment equal to the amount they would have made if their contributions had been invested in company stock plus a 15% add-on. The plan rules were so incredibly arcane that the outsourcing provider had to build a custom system to support it. That was the least of the problems.

Problem No. 1: During the one-year contribution period, the stock price dropped more than 15%. This meant that everyone lost money.

Problem No. 2: The company had made a decision to convert currency only at the end of the one-year period. During this same year, the currency in many Southeast Asian countries dropped dramatically against the U.S. dollar. In one case, the combination of the drop in currency and the drop in stock price resulted in participants' final U.S. dollar payment being almost equal to the first month's contribution they had made. Essentially, those participants lost every penny they contributed in months two through twelve. Needless to say, this did not result in the motivation and retention impact hoped for by the company.

Lessons

Sometimes a company that wants to do right by its employees will bend over backward to design a compensation benefit plan that does what they want. And, while it's important to understand that template equity compensation plans may not fit your company's goals, it can be very risky to design something so unique that small details result in big consequences.

When designing or customizing a plan, be sure to consider the following:

- How will the plan be administered? Will plan administration require new or customized technology? Will the cost of the technology present a budgetary challenge that undermines the benefit the plan intends to provide?
- What is the worst thing that could happen? When trying to do something good for our employees, sometimes we only look toward

the happy ending. It's important for risk mitigation to consider the darker "what if" questions.

- Can the plan be implemented in the same way for domestic and foreign business units, or will there be additional considerations for the foreign entities, like currency conversion?

Don't Forget to Do the Math

Fred Whittlesey, Hay Group

A subsidiary of a Fortune 50 company, which represented a tiny proportion of the parent company's overall business, had been acquired. To continue to retain and motivate the executive team, a phantom stock program was implemented. The parameters seemed to make sense, on the surface. Because many private, pre-IPO companies in this industry would set aside 10% to 15% of shares in a long-term incentive plan, the company decided to dedicate the equivalent of 15% of company value to the phantom plan.

The phantom shares were valued assuming that in a comparable public company the shares would trade for 12 times earnings, so shares were valued on that basis, but discounted for the private status to a multiple of 8.

At the end of the first year of operation, an astute accountant noted that 12% of the gross earnings multiplied by 8 resulted in 120% of the company's net profit being allocated to the executive phantom stock plan. Worse, because the plan provision that allowed plan termination stated that no outstanding grants could be modified if such modification would reduce the value to the participant, those first grants continued to live on and accrue value for their full five-year terms.

Lessons

Sometimes equity horror stories result from plans implemented in lieu of equity but referencing how actual equity would operate. In practice, cash can rarely, if ever, truly replicate the dynamics of equity, and attempting to do so can be prohibitively expensive.

It takes only 30 minutes to do a math problem that could have saved this company from the embarrassment of making this costly error.

What Goes Up...

Jim Sillery, Buck Consultants

It was the 1990s and the scent of excitement was in the air. Bill Jones had recently been hired to run ABC Corp., a privately held, Midwestern manufacturing company with about $400 million in annual revenues. Although performance had been flat for the past few years, Jones saw nothing but opportunity. With the full commitment of the company's shareholders, he brought on his handpicked leadership team, people he had worked with, knew, and trusted. After their three-day strategic planning meeting, he was full of confidence in future success.

Still, something was missing. He had seen firms in Silicon Valley use executive compensation programs to achieve growth and value. He needed something like that here. He needed something that would align everyone to the business plan; something that would hold out a carrot big enough to get everyone's attention.

He met with his human resources director to review the compensation programs and was not impressed. Salaries were competitive and the annual bonus was OK, but there was no upside to the program, no sizzle. The problem was the long-term plan. He wanted something that could provide significant rewards for all of the value that they would create. The current Performance Unit Plan was too boring. Even the name, PUP, was boring. There was a proposal on the table to consider a book-value plan, but that was boring, too. That is definitely not what they would do in Silicon Valley.

Jones called his friend Bob Smith, who had done some work as a compensation consultant out West to get some fresh thinking. He and Bob kicked around some ideas. He liked what he heard. They would grant stock appreciation rights (SARs), just like in Silicon Valley. To focus executives on the financials, the grants would be for synthetic equity whose value was based on a multiple of earnings before interest, taxes, depreciation, and amortization (EBITDA). But to make the plan really dynamic, they would also value the shares using a multiple based on the changes in the Standard & Poor's 500 stock index. He had enough shareholder votes behind him to guarantee approval, so all that really was left was to implement the plan. It was rolled out for plan year 1995.

It was during plan year 1998 that the CFO called an emergency meeting. While the company's EBITDA had shown slow but steady growth, the S&P 500 had doubled, going from 600 to 1,200. Because of the S&P 500 multiplier, the SARs' settlement price had also shot up, creating an unfunded liability that now threatened to bankrupt the company. The executives did not want to give up their gains, and the shareholders did not want to pay. The outcome seemed obvious. The next round of calls went out to the attorneys.

Lessons

There are two lessons here. First, there is no "one-size-fits-all" approach for long-term incentive compensation design. What works in one industry may not work in another. In fact, my experience shows that one plan may not work for two companies in the same industry if their work cultures are materially different. The second lesson is that you can never take plan design at its face value. You have to "stress test" a plan by using what-if scenarios to determine if there is the potential for unintended consequences like, in this case, paying for someone else's performance and bankrupting the company.

A speaker on a panel I recently attended recommended a three-prong design stress test that should reveal almost any problems prior to implementing the plan. Here is his suggestion for stress testing:

- *Best case.* Run the numbers showing what would happen if the very best outcome were achieved on every target measurement. Do this for each vesting tranche.
- *Neutral case.* Run the numbers for what would happen if absolutely nothing changed from the grant date to each vesting tranche date.
- *Worst case.* Run the numbers on what would happen if the very worst outcome was realized on every target measurement. Do this for each vesting tranche.

To this suggestion I would add that when you have multiple measurement factors, as in the case above, it would be wise to test additional combination scenarios, like this:

- Best-case factor 1 to:
  - Best-case factor 2
  - Neutral-case factor 2
  - Worst-case factor 2
- Neutral-case factor 1 to:
  - Best-case factor 2
  - Neutral-case factor 2
  - Worst-case factor 2
- Worst-case factor 1 to:
  - Best-case factor 2
  - Neutral-case factor 2
  - Worst-case factor 2

Stress testing is especially important for performance plans and for any plans that have unusual terms or multiple measurement factors. I highly recommend testing a few wildly unlikely scenarios because, as the story above points out, almost anything really can happen. It's so much better to catch these surprises before the plan is implemented than have to explain to shareholders that poor design has caused a serious crisis.

Following the Herd—the Wrong Herd

Fred Whittlesey, Hay Group

When the market downturn of 2008 drove many companies' option grants underwater, option exchanges became an attractive solution. ABC Company's outstanding options were far underwater, so company leadership decided to pursue an option exchange early in the market downturn.

Due to a steep decline in share price, the calculated value of the underwater options was minimal, resulting in high exchange ratios in the option exchange. Employees, on average, received one option at a new at-the-market grant price for ten underwater options. Many employees refused to participate, including one executive who said he refused out of a combination of "protest and disgust."

The company followed the advice of the consulting firm and pursued a cookie-cutter value-for-value exchange, although it could have been more generous even to the point of a straight one-for-one repricing because, as luck would have it, ABC Company had no need to obtain the blessing of any of the proxy advisory firms or any major institutional shareholders.

A few months later, the company's stock price had declined further, and the employees found themselves with a much smaller number of underwater options than they held before the exchange, with no associated value to shareholders. Worse, the company had agreed to retire the original exchanged options in another consultant-suggested cookie-cutter provision to satisfy advisors and institutions and, as a result, had a significantly reduced share pool available to make additional grants. Having run out of shares as a result of using available shares for new hires and being cash constrained, the company suffered on both hiring and retention and ended up being sold at a price that created no gains from any outstanding options.

Lessons

There is a reason that subject-matter experts are called "consultants." Their recommendations are guidance, not gospel. They are only as good as the forethought that goes into them, and company management is responsible for analyzing the likely effect of the recommendations before signing off on them. It is never in a company's best interest to adopt a strategy just because everyone else is doing it—not in business and not in equity compensation.

In this case, upon receiving the consultant's recommendation, the company should have:

- run a best-case scenario with the company's stock price rising;
- run a neutral-case scenario with the company's stock price staying the same; and
- run a worst-case scenario with the company's stock price falling (as it actually did).

It then could have evaluated the impact of each of those scenarios over a six-month and twelve-month period on both the structure of the option plan and on the morale of the employees. Such an analysis would have made the company's fallacy in retiring the original exchanged options clear ahead of time.

Despite management's desire to do a quick and easy exchange of underwater options, the failure to consider the impact on the employee base and to take employee feedback into consideration where appropriate before taking action produced significantly counterproductive results.

The Danger of Round Numbers

Fred Whittlesey, Hay Group

Although it is not as volatile as high fashion, equity compensation plan design also goes through trends, largely influenced by the state of the economy, shareholder satisfaction, government regulation, and other such considerations. One year, total shareholder return (TSR) was a hot topic. The general interpretation of TSR is that it is a basis for comparing the performance of different companies' stocks and shares over time. It combines share price appreciation and dividends paid to show the total return to the shareholder. The absolute size of the TSR will vary with stock market fluctuations, but the relative position reflects the market perception of overall performance relative to a reference group.

One consulting firm's interpretation of TSR was premised on the idea that not only should relative stock price performance outperform the median of the peer group over a three-year period, but also that absolute stock price appreciation for that specific industry should always be a minimum of 10% per year over that period regardless of the company size.

In the toughest year ever in its industry, XYZ Co. put in a stellar performance and significantly outperformed its entire peer group. Yet its star producers received no reward for their outstanding efforts. Why? Because the performance awards contained the indiscriminate 10%-per-year threshold that had been recommended to the company, and XYZ Co.'s relative TSR was 2%—enough to outperform the company's peers, which all had negative TSRs as a result of the broad market decline, but not to meet the arbitrary benchmark set by the consulting firm.

Lessons

Using realistic numbers for market returns is essential. Even without the possibility of unprecedented economic situations, sharp market increases, or sharp market declines, it would be inconceivable that a nice round number like 10% would ever possibly be the appropriate performance target for every company across an industry. Very few companies can realistically expect to see stock price growth of 10% a year. Simplistic solutions are often appealing, but their results are often simply ineffective. Furthermore, when times are good, it's easy to pretend that will always be the case, but even if you expect a future filled with sunshine, run through rainy-day scenarios anyway, and consider whether your optimistic plan design could leave the employees you want to keep seeking shelter somewhere else.

You're So Special

Fred Whittlesey, Hay Group

Making someone a cake is a great way to customize what is essentially the same for every person and every situation—no matter what you do to it, it's still cake. The fact that you took the time to customize it for a special person on his or her special day makes it a memorable and appreciated gesture.

The same level of customization with stock options, however, will not create the same warm fuzzies.

ABC Co. had a hands-on CEO with a strong interest in compensation decisions. Over and above the monetary value of the options, she wanted each employee to understand the level of thought put into granting their specific equity award. Thus, to demonstrate her interest in her employees, she individually designed the vesting schedules for the top 300 employees and executives, resulting in 300 unique vesting schedules that were crafted specifically to ensure that at any point in time, no employee saw a dip in his or her unvested option gains (assuming the options were in the money).

The stock plan administration group was, of course, horrified by the thought of manually entering and administering 300 unique schedules. The group pushed back and ultimately reached an agreement that implemented the spirit of the CEO's idea but with a mere 60 unique vesting schedules, with vesting schedules that were as long as 10 years, and with odd numbers of options vesting per year (not percentages but actual numbers of options).

Even this simplified approach couldn't avoid the inevitable consequences of bringing individual-level customization into an area where it doesn't belong:

- The workload for the stock administration group was increased by over 20%, making the administrators unhappy.
- The HR department saw a similar increase in the form of extra communication to explain to employees the unique features of each and every grant, making the department both unhappy and frustrated.
- The employees were confused by the unusual award terms, and became discontented as they learned of others' more favorable vesting schedules.

Lessons

Equity compensation is not the equivalent of a birthday gift; it is an employee benefit that:

- will be talked about among employees no matter what company policy says about not comparing salaries;
- will be administered by company staff who must maximize the efficiency of their time in order to best serve the company; and
- will be perceived as less valuable by an employee in direct relation to how difficult it is for the employee to understand it.

Final word: Demonstrations of individual recognition belong in performance reviews; an equity compensation award made concurrent with a good performance review is wonderful, but make the award terms standard and both the employee and the administration staff will be as grateful as you had hoped for.

Unclear Documents Cost Company

Achaessa James, NCEO

Graphic Packaging Holding Co. v. Humphrey, No. 10-12015, 2010 WL 4608775 (11th Cir. Nov. 16, 2010) presents a good example of "What would you do?" and why that type of question should never arise in connection with an equity compensation plan. The plan really must leave nothing to chance. This is especially true when updating existing documents to comply with new regulations. Internal Revenue Code Section 409A, and other regulations like it that allow for time to bring existing documents into compliance, created the perfect opportunity for a company to modify existing documents without thinking through all of the related details.

In *Graphic Packaging*, the company had an equity compensation plan in place that used restricted stock units (RSUs). While the president and CEO was in an active employment relationship with the company, he received an award of RSUs that were to be paid out one-half in cash and one-half in shares of company stock. In compliance with 2009 amendments to Section 409A,[1] the president met the definition of "specified employees"[2] and when he retired at the end of 2007 the payout of his vested RSUs was delayed by at least six months in accordance with that statute. On June 30, 2008, the company paid the retired executive approximately $1.2 million for the cash portion of the vested RSUs. The payout was based on the value of the company's stock on the date of his retirement, December 31, 2007.

In 2008, the company completed a review of the payout and concluded that the cash portion of the award should have been based on the value of the stock on the date of the payout (June 30, 2008), instead of the date of retirement (December 31, 2007). That conclusion, however,

---

1. This applies to amounts deferred on and after January 1, 2005. Proposed regulations were issued under Section 409A on October 4, 2005, and final regulations were issued on April 17, 2007. The final regulations generally became effective on January 1, 2009, and before then a plan had to be operated in "good faith compliance" with Section 409A and prior guidance issued by the IRS.

2. Internal Revenue Code Section 409A requires that any deferred compensation payment that is made on account of separation from service to a "specified employee" of a public company be delayed for at least six months following separation from service.

was not based on anything in the plan or grant documents. Indeed, the documentation was silent on when to value deferred payouts.

The plot thickens. Since the stock price had decreased significantly in value between the original payout date and the adjusted payout date, the company sent the retired executive a request for repayment of $540,000, citing the overpayment as a result of "administrative error." You're probably shaking your head right now. So did the retired executive, and he refused to pay. And the company sued him. It went all the way to the Eleventh Circuit Court of Appeals.

In the end, the court held that a failure of plan documents to specifically state when an award of cash-settled RSUs was to be valued for the purpose of determining the amount to be paid out was a "notable" omission. As a result, because recovery of amounts previously paid out was involved, the burden was on the company to produce sufficient evidence to support a change of valuation date. Although the appellate court found that the company's assertion that the cash portion of the RSU should be valued as of the payout date was reasonable, it held that in the absence of a clear valuation mandate in the award documents, the company could not provide sufficient evidence to support a finding that the original payout was a mistake.

Lessons

This case contains several important lessons:

- Always review the language in plans and grant documentation to ensure that the terms and conditions clearly reflect and expressly state the company's intent with regard to all aspects of the award.
- When modifying plan and award documents to conform to new regulations, take the time to consider the consequences of those modifications on existing awards.
- Where there is a regulatory mandate that allows the company flexibility in execution, make sure that the execution implemented is in alignment with the company's interests.
- And, as usual, it's best if these analyses are done before a problem arises.

Let's not forget one of the biggest lessons—the cost of litigation. A Google search for "*cost of litigation*" and *2011* results in over 62,000 hits. As of this writing only one month of 2011 had passed, so if even only 10% of those hits were pertinent, there were over 6,000 mentions of the cost of litigation in January 2011. The costs associated with a legal action are so high, there is a magazine fully dedicated to the problem called "Alternatives to the High Cost of Litigation" that has been successfully published since 1983. According to a February 1, 2008, paper published on The Metropolitan Corporate Counsel site by the president of eLawForum, "No one knows exactly what the Fortune 500 spend on litigation. Being privy to information from a significant number of Fortune 500 corporations in a wide range of businesses, eLawForum estimates the total cost of litigation to be $210 billion, equivalent to one-third of the after-tax profit of the Fortune 500."[3]

Coming from a legal background, it is relatively easy for me to provide a partial summary of the cost items involved in litigation:

- *Attorney fees.* This is obvious, but let's look at the detail to get a better understanding:
  - *Plaintiff's attorney.* In this case, the company would pay first to consult its regular corporate attorney. Because it is a case involving the tax code, a tax lawyer would be consulted, along with an employment law attorney because the case involves an equity compensation plan. In each of these departments, it would be likely that there was a senior attorney consulted who would assign a junior associate or a paralegal to do the research work and make recommendations. Once the decision was made to go to trial, the case would then be referred to the law firm's litigation department. A senior litigator would be assigned to the case, along with at least one junior attorney, a paralegal, and perhaps an investigator. If a case goes to appeal like this one did, then there are also trial lawyers who specialize in appellate cases, again usually a senior/junior/paralegal team assignment.

---

3. "Fortune 500: The Total Cost of Litigation Estimated at One-Third Profits," *The Metropolitan Corporate Counsel,* http://www.metrocorpcounsel.com/current.php?artType=view&artMonth=February&artYear=2008&EntryNo=7862.

So, in total, approximately 12 legal professionals would work on the case with hourly billable rates from $200 to $600 or more depending upon the specific law firm and the experience of each professional.

- *Defendant's attorney.* The executive in this case would have to consult his own experts and assemble a litigation team. So, in total, another approximately 12 legal professionals would work on the case with hourly billable rates from $200 to $600 or more depending upon the specific law firm and the experience of each professional.

- *Processing fees.* Fees in this category would include:
  - *Filing fees* with the court for initiating the case, for filing procedural motions, for ordering trial transcripts, and for various and sundry other interactions with the court—and at each level of appeal, if the case is appealed. These are generally nominal fees, but they can mount up depending upon the level of activity. As an example, at the time of this writing the filing fee in Orange County, California, is $395 each for the initial complaint and the initial answer, $500 for a motion for summary judgment (common where the facts of the case and the law seem to be straightforward), $40 for most other motions, and $750 for initial fees to the appellate court.
  - *Service of process* to any parties to the case or witnesses to the facts. The method of service may range from a certifiable delivery method or personal service by a process server if a party or witness is unwilling to accept notice of the complaint or a summons through his or her attorney; personal service can sometimes cost hundreds of dollars if the person is very uncooperative.
  - *Trial fees* must also be paid when the case goes to trial. For example, again in Orange County, fees include a $150 first day jury deposit, then daily fees as set by the court depending upon how many days of trial, and $250 per half day for a single court reporter (there can be more than one court reporter depending upon the complexity of the case).

- *Discovery costs.* Discovery is the evidentiary aspect of the case. A 2008 survey on civil litigation costs revealed, "On average, 45-50 percent of respondents' civil litigation costs in 2007 related to discovery activities."[4] Discovery is where each set of attorneys sends the other set of attorneys a long list of questions that require answers, copies of documents or other evidence, or both. Even in a case that appears to be clear cut, discovery requests are often voluminous and specifically designed to be burdensome. Discovery costs can be broken down into several activities—prepare, review, research, respond, produce, and analyze.
  - *Prepare.* Discovery is begun by preparing documents called interrogatories and requests for production. The interrogatories are questions that must be answered, and the requests for production ask for the responding side to provide the asking side with copies of documents or other evidence that supports the responding side's position. Both of these documents exist in every law firm in a template format that is then tailored to the facts of each case. The preparation time would be included in the legal professional's billable time above and would follow a process similar to this: The paralegal is asked to customize the template documents, which are then passed to the junior associate who customizes them further, while at the same time the investigator is gathering information specific to the case and suggesting additional customization, which the associate or paralegal then incorporates into the documents. The senior partner then reviews the documents and either edits or approves, and then the documents are served on the opposing party.
  - *Review.* Though the questions asked and the documents requested are supposed to pertain to the facts of the case, the sending party often includes non-applicable questions, either because the template was not well customized or, as

4. "Data from 2008 on discovery costs in litigation and some important metrics," *Law Department Management*, January 26, 2011, http://www.lawdepartmentmanagementblog.com/law_department_management/2011/01/data-from-2008-on-discovery-costs-in-litigation-and-some-important-metrics.html.

some assert, to solicit prejudicial answers or to simply make the response process more cumbersome. Upon receipt, the discovery request will first be reviewed by either the senior partner or junior associate to determine which of the requests merit real responses and which can be denied as not applicable. Those requests marked for response are then categorized by the type of information sought and whether that information is readily ascertainable or whether it will require information not on hand, including documents and other forms of physical evidence.

— *Research.* Requests that require evidentiary responses or unavailable factual information will require research to formulate an appropriate response. The documentary requests will often be passed to the responding client for assembly of those documents by an in-house person or, if it is a very important case or very voluminous request, a team of attorneys, paralegals, and researchers may be stationed at the client's premises or data warehouse to comb through and analyze all available documentation for pertinence to the case. Either way, the company is now involved in contributing often significant staff hours in locating and providing potentially responsive physical and digital evidence. I add digital evidence here because email and other digital correspondence, including blogs, discussion forums, etc., are discoverable materials, and electronic discovery (or e-discovery) has become a significant and time consuming aspect of civil litigation discovery. Indeed, that same 2008 survey reports, "When used, e-discovery vendors accounted for, on average, 10-12 percent of total costs."[5]

— *Respond.* While the research is being conducted, the original requests are being prepared for response. The requests are usually received in hardcopy form, often dozens and sometimes hundreds of pages. The document will go to the law firm's word processing department for scanning, clean-up, and conversion to a digital document. An attorney will draft

5. "Data from 2008 on discovery costs in litigation and some important metrics," note 4 above.

the direct responses, crafting answers that give information in a way that still protects the client. Even those requests that will be denied must be denied on appropriate legal grounds, and those responses require an appropriate level of legalese to cite the reason for denial. The responsive document will go through many states of draft, review, and polish before being finalized and involve every attorney and paralegal assigned to the case. The final document will be printed out and signed by the senior attorney and the client. These written responses are often hundreds of pages long.

— *Produce.* Once the responsive evidence has been identified, there is a cost to reproduce that evidence for delivery to the requesting party—you most certainly won't give up your originals. This used to be the part of discovery that cost thousands and thousands of dollars in copying and reproduction fees. With the advent of electronic discovery, much discovery is now delivered in digital form, and trees are spared, but the cost of discovery remains the same or even increases as the depth and breadth of possibly responsive data has exploded to include emails on computers and laptops, text messages on cellphones and PDAs, and on and on into the digital horizon. The paralegal and researcher will coordinate and catalog the evidentiary documents, cross-referencing them to the appropriate discovery request; if the evidence is only in hard copy it will get scanned and aggregated with existing digital evidence, and it will be put all together in a neat package that is then delivered along with the printed-out written responses to the requesting party.

— *Analyze.* Once the requesting party receives the responses, the answers and evidence are analyzed and a new round of discovery requests begins. The analysis is conducted by the attorneys; the paralegals are given the task of identifying and tracking every piece of paper associated with the discovery.

And, as with attorney fees, discovery is an activity that both sides of the case participate in equally, so double whatever your wildest guess may be at the costs that have accumulated so far.

I include the estimates for both sides here because frequently the losing side will have to pay the prevailing side's attorney fees, so, either way, one side often bears the economic burden of both prosecuting and defending.

Keeping the cost of litigation in mind, I want you to ask yourself a couple of hypothetical questions:

- What is your wild guess of the cost of this litigation on both sides?
- What is the relationship between that cost and the $540,000 the company was suing for?
- Was it worth it to the company to pursue this litigation? Even if it had won?
- Might the lawsuit have been pursued by the company, in part, to avoid a shareholder suit against the company?
- If a plan administrator in such a situation had prepared a comprehensive summary of plan terms and noticed this missing data point before the payout was made, could this litigation have been avoided?

These are just hypothetical questions, but, considering the current economy, reducing legal fees can be an attractive and relatively painless way to rescue "one-third of the after-tax profit of the Fortune 500"[6] and keep it in the company's coffers.

6. "Data from 2008 on discovery costs in litigation and some important metrics," note 4 above.

Chapter 2

Administration, Process, and Policy

Once the plan is in place, the next appropriate step is to put in place policies and processes that make the administration of the plan as easy as possible. This step is usually skipped, and the board goes directly into granting awards. Then the person charged with administering the plan goes into panic mode to get the awards out in a timely manner and pretty much stays in a panic forever after, and you end up with stories worthy of publishing in books like this.

Okay, that's an exaggeration. But it's close.

Policies and procedures are necessary for the comfort of the company, the administrator, and the award recipients. If the plan is administered in a consistent manner, everybody knows what to expect, and there will be fewer cracks for exceptions to creep out of and fewer costly surprises for the company.

Setting up good policies and procedures is not difficult but, again, you will want to look at whatever templates may be offered by your service providers to ensure that they meet your needs. If someone in-house develops the policies and procedures, check them to make sure that they cover all the bases. Make sure that everything is in writing and that there are quality checks and approvals. Remember to include procedures for essential communications between internal stakeholders like the equity administrator and Payroll and Finance and Legal and HR and . . . well, you get the picture. There are so many moving parts to equity administration that well-constructed policies and procedures will be an essential roadmap for everyone involved.

The ESPP Dilemma

Dan Walter, Performensation Consulting

An employee stock purchase plan (ESPP) is a great way for a company to allow its employees to purchase stock, usually at a discount, and build an employee ownership culture. Section 423 ESPP stock is tax-qualified and allows employees to later sell the stock and treat the gain on the sale largely as capital gain instead of ordinary income. That's nice, right? But, like many gifts, there are some strings attached. If the participant holds the stock for both two years after the grant date (the original offer date) and one year after the purchase date, then any sale or transfer is a qualifying disposition, which means the participant must pay ordinary income taxes on the lesser of (1) the difference between the stock price on the first day of the offering period and what the purchase price would have been if the purchase price had been set that day (even if it wasn't), or (2) the actual gain on the sale of stock. The remainder of the sale proceeds are taxed at lower capital gains tax rates. If the stock is sold or transferred before the holding period requirement has been met, then it is a disqualifying disposition; the company must report the gain as ordinary income to the participant, and no tax benefit is available to the participant. In a disqualifying disposition, the company is allowed a tax deduction equal to the amount the employee must recognize as ordinary income, which is common in most income-producing situations. Qualifying dispositions are unusual in this regard because companies are not allowed a tax deduction for any income generated in a qualifying disposition of ESPP shares.

The company must track stock purchased in an ESPP until the employee or ex-employee (the "participant") sells or transfers the stock. It sounds simple, but it means that a company could be tracking stock for many years, even if it is held by participants who are no longer employees of the company.

Years ago I had a client who had a Section 423 qualified ESPP. To comply with the tracking requirements, the company made it a policy to survey each participant once in the year following the purchase. If there was no response to the survey, the company made the assumption that the shares were sold in the year after the purchase and, thus, in a disqualifying disposition. The company reported the assumed sales proceeds as ordinary income on the participant's W-2 and took the related corporate tax deduction generated by the disqualifying disposition.

This tracking policy was followed for several years before an ex-employee participant sold his ESPP shares after meeting all Section 423 holding periods and filed his tax return declaring the stock sale as a qualifying disposition. The participant was audited. The mismatch between what the company had reported years earlier and what the participant reported for the current year was identified, and the IRS turned to the company for answers.

In the end, the IRS fined the company heavily for taking tax deductions that it wasn't entitled to, and forced it to set up a program in which every participant from the prior six years of purchases was re-surveyed. Quarterly surveys had to be sent to all participants (employees and ex-employees) until every share had been accounted for. Overall it took an additional seven years to complete all of the survey requirements—13 years, in total, from the beginning of the first affected offering to the day when all ESPP shares sold during the six-year period had been accounted for.

Lessons

In retrospect, it was a whole lot of work required because someone wanted to simplify processes but did not consider the repercussions. While administrative efficiency is an admirable goal, shortcuts often fall short of meeting regulatory requirements. Steps that could have been taken to avoid this situation:

- When regulations have been set forth, it's important to follow them to the letter, even if it feels like a hardship.
- Having a qualified professional design or review administrative procedures is just as important as having a qualified professional design the plan.
- Having a qualified professional administering the plan is no longer a luxury in this highly regulated industry.

ESPP Contribution Carryover

Robyn Shutak, NASPP

One of the elements that make tax-qualified ESPPs so attractive is the egalitarian nature of their "equal rights and privileges" provisions. With very few exceptions, every employee must be treated the same and have the same opportunity to participate in the ESPP. Every time. It would seem an easy-enough rule to remember, but unless an administrator has been properly trained and actually knows the tax rules that go along with ESPP administration, it's easy for things to go awry.

An experienced plan administrator joined a mid-size biotech company just prior to the first purchase date under a new offering under the company's tax-qualified ESPP. During the course of preparing for the upcoming purchase date, the administrator asked for and received a contribution summary for the period from the payroll department and immediately noticed that contributions appeared high for a number of the participants. After doing some investigative work, the administrator discovered that the prior administrator had allowed employees who previously exceeded the $25,000 limit under the prior offering to carry forward the excess contributions to the current offering—in effect making a lump sum contribution to the new offering. The administrator also discovered that new enrollees in the current offering had not also been given the opportunity to make lump sum contributions to the plan.

The only action available to take was adjusting contributions and issuing refunds of the excess contributions prior to the purchase date. Communicating the reason for the refund to the affected participants and corporate executives also took a lot of explaining.

Lessons

There are some good lessons here for new and experienced plan administrators:

- New plan administrators should be educated in the rules that govern the administration of tax-qualified plans.
- Even if you're an experienced administrator and are sure you know the rules, double-check when an unusual situation arises, and check

with your professional peers or expert advisors if you are unsure how to proceed.

- Plan administrators should insist on receiving ESPP contribution data from payroll regularly throughout a purchase period and verify it for accuracy.

Listen to your gut and experience; if something doesn't look or feel right, it usually isn't.

Zombie Options

Mike Stevens, Alston & Bird LLP

A small manufacturing company maintains a long-term incentive plan under which it has issued options to employees. Pursuant to the terms of the plan and the award agreements, the options have a 10-year term but lapse 90 days after termination of employment, if earlier.

A longtime employee is granted options, satisfies the vesting conditions, and retires from the company. Six months after retirement, the employee sends in a form and a check to exercise the options. The plan administrator wants to do the "right thing" and would rather not have to inform the former employee that he can no longer exercise the award.

Unfortunately, from a legal standpoint, the option has expired by its terms. It has, so to speak, kicked the bucket. This is an ex-option.

Lessons

Most options have several different "termination" dates. The first is the overall expiration date. For example, a 10-year option expires on the 10th anniversary of grant. That expiration date cannot be changed or extended—to do so would be akin to granting a new option.

The other termination dates are lapse events. As noted in the example above, these are deadlines that will terminate the option before the expiration date, if some event has occurred. It is common to see a lapse provision of one year for death or disability and 30, 60, or 90 days for termination for any other reason (other than for cause, which typically terminates the options immediately).

It is often possible to extend the lapse date of an option. Under 409A of the Internal Revenue Code, such an extension will not be treated as a material modification of the award, as long as the lapse period does not extend beyond the original expiration date. For example, if you issue 7-year options, the employee resigns 6.5 years after the date of grant, and the award provides for a 90-day lapse provision, you cannot extend the lapse period for an entire year. But extending that option an additional 90 days so that it expires on the 7-year anniversary of the grant date normally would be fine. Be sure to check with your accountants before approving an extension of a lapse period so that you understand what accounting issues may arise, if any.

And remember that extensions don't work once the lapse period has expired. Reviving a dead option is the same thing as granting a new, discounted option. That would require board approval and raises difficult issues under Section 409A if the option is in the money. It also may raise issues under your plan and certain securities exemptions, which often contemplate that new grants will be made to current employees and other service providers.

While not technically required, it is always good practice to give employees a written reminder about the option lapse provision when they leave the company. If you want to be really nice, follow that up with another friendly notice when the exercise period is drawing to a close. That avoids the rather unpleasant spectacle of watching a former colleague lose out on potentially significant gain because he or she missed the exercise deadline. Remember, though, any notice policy must be consistently applied to all grants and all grant recipients to avoid any legal claims of preference or discrimination.

There is no easy way to handle zombie options. The best way to avoid them is with prior notice, reminders, and clear communication. That way, if a wayward exercise notice comes your way, you can say with a clean conscience, "I'm sorry, but your option has lapsed and can no longer be exercised."

Get with the Plan

Mike Stevens, Alston & Bird LLP

In 2005, a company adopted a stock option plan that included a change in control accelerator. Under the plan definitions, a change in control would occur if, following a merger, the shareholders of the company held less than a 60% interest in the resulting company. The company granted options under this plan for several years.

When the plan started running low on available shares, the company decided to adopt a new incentive plan in 2009. The board decided that the old change in control threshold was too easily triggered and changed it in the new plan, so that a change in control would occur if the shareholders retained less than a majority of the shares in the resulting company.

While the company would have preferred to have a uniform change in control definition apply to all outstanding awards, any such change to the options under the initial plan would require consent of all of the holders. Accordingly, the company decided to leave the 2005 plan unchanged and to allow the existing options to remain subject to the old change in control definition.

Following the adoption of the 2009 plan, the compensation committee continued to grant options. The grant resolutions did not specify which plan the new awards were to be issued under, but the stock plan administrator decided to make full use of all the shares under the 2005 plan and continued to grant awards under that plan until the share reserve was exhausted. Only after that were new awards then allocated to the 2009 plan.

Some time later, several employees left the company and forfeited their options under the 2005 plan. According to the terms of the plan, these shares again became available for grant, and the stock plan administrator issued the next few options under the 2005 plan, again to exhaust the share reserve. Over time, there was little rhyme or reason as to why certain employees received 2005 plan options and why others received 2009 plan options—the administrator simply used up shares in the old plan whenever they became available. The result was a more or less random allocation of plan shares after 2009.

In 2010, the company was approached by a similarly sized company interested in a "merger of equals." As a result of the merger, the company's shareholders would control approximately 53% of the equity in the resulting company. While preparing the option schedules for the due diligence report, the stock plan administrator was horrified to realize that, upon closing of the merger, options would accelerate under the terms of the 2005 plan but would not accelerate under the 2009 plan. As a result, options granted to different employees in the same year would have completely different merger treatment based upon the allocation of the 2005 plan shares.

In order to avoid this disparate treatment among its employees, the board of the larger company decided to accelerate everyone's awards. Employees at the smaller company did not like the fact that the larger company's employees were getting their awards accelerated, so its board decided to accelerate all of their awards, as well. This caused a great deal of heartburn at both companies and resulted in a significant expense.

Lessons

Any time a new plan has terms that are inconsistent with grants made under an old plan, it is best to cut off grants under the old plan all at once. It is much easier to track the awards and to explain to employees and investors that all awards issued prior to a certain date were under the old plan and all subsequent awards were under the new plan.

The efficient use of plan shares is a good idea, but rather than dip back into the old plan as awards are forfeited, it is better practice to pass board resolutions instructing that:

1. No awards will be issued under the old plan after the new plan is in place, and
2. The number of shares authorized under the new plan is X shares, plus a number of shares that would have again become available for grant under the old plan due to forfeiture or cancellation (not to exceed Y shares).

More importantly, where two plans are in place, it is imperative that the compensation committee indicate which plan an award is being granted under. Where the terms of the plans differ (particularly around a provision as important as a change in control accelerator), the choice of plans directly impacts the terms of the awards, and only the committee has the authority to set the terms of the awards.

In this case, while the stock plan administrator did not have corporate authority to set the terms of the options by allocating them between the plans, the employees had all been given stock option agreements denoting the plan under which their awards were issued. While these award agreements were prepared by the stock plan administrator, they were fixed with the facsimile signature of the CEO. The company realized that it would be difficult to get all of the employees who had received options in 2009 and later that were issued under the 2005 plan to consent to the stricter change in control treatment under the 2009 plan and felt compelled to extend the vesting acceleration to all employees.

Not-So-Golden Oldies

Achaessa James, NCEO

As with most start-ups, staff members are expected to fill multiple roles until the company starts generating revenue. A candidate for office manager of a start-up company was a corporate paralegal looking to change professions. During the interview, the CEO asked if the candidate would be willing to take charge of administering the company's stock option plan, and with agreement on that point, the deal was sealed in late 2004.

Upon beginning her new position, the office manager made a thorough review of all available corporate governance documents and grant documents to ensure that everything reconciled–bylaws, articles of incorporation, amendments to both, board minutes and consents, founders stock agreements, option awards, and the spreadsheets kept for tracking options and stock. The company had been founded as an S corporation in 2000 with an issuance of founders stock, had reincorporated in 2002 as a C corporation with conversion of the founders stock and an additional issuance of preferred stock to the founder to retire some corporate debt, and had done a single round of option grants to the original team of employees in 2003. Some of the staff had left the company and exercised their vested options, and some had simply left and forfeited their awards, but the bulk of the team was still intact and had met the first year tranche vesting and subsequent monthly vesting. The office manager found only a few discrepancies that were easily reconciled. She explained to the CEO that beginning in 2006 the options would need to be valued and expensed and that putting everything into a Web-based administration program would be the most efficient way to track issuances and do the required expensing calculations. The CEO agreed, and the new database was established.

In early 2005 the CEO, acting as sole director, authorized a round of option and restricted stock awards to a small group of new hires. As the year progressed the company switched corporate counsel to a well-known firm in the spring, then in the summer amended the bylaws to allow up to five directors, and added two new directors and three advisors. The new board authorized option awards for themselves, the advisors, and the most recent new hires. Corporate counsel prepared all of the minutes for the board meetings, and the office manager updated the equity compensation database as authorized.

In early 2006, the 2005 options met their first cliff vesting, and some of the employees exercised their ISO options because the stock price was still very low. A couple of exiting executives also exercised large vested ISO awards. In the summer of 2006, the company reached agreement with a venture capital firm to do a Series A round of preferred stock in exchange for an investment of private capital. All was going well until the law firm documenting the deal did a corporate governance review and found that when the original corporate counsel did the 2002 reincorporation as a C Corp they had used a decade-old template for the amended articles of incorporation to effect the addition of the preferred stock that retired the founders debt. The template included language that increased the number of directors "to a minimum of three and a maximum of five." The language had gone unnoticed by the CEO, original corporate counsel, the office manager, and replacement counsel.

After much discussion, the deal lawyers concluded that, even though the change had not been mentioned in the board minutes, nor reflected in the bylaws, and had not been the intention of the sole authorizing board member at the time of the original transaction, the change in the number of directors was valid and that all actions taken by the CEO as a sole director between 2002 and mid-2005 (when the new directors were appointed and the bylaws formally amended) were invalid.

The end result was that the employee options authorized in 2003 and early 2005 were voided and had to be re-issued at current fair market value. It wasn't much of a change to the 2005 awards, but because the CEO had decided to wait until after closing the Series A investment round to update the valuation, the strike price on the original 2003 awards had increased by 25x according to the post-closing stock valuation. Making the original staff "whole" in this situation was not possible because it would have a negative impact on the allocation of the option pool reserve that was supposed to last two years after the venture financing. On top of the impact to the option awards, since the underlying awards had been voided, all exercises were also invalid, resulting in the necessity of re-documenting all of the exercises as direct purchases of common stock, backing everything out of the stock administration software and putting it back in. Needless to say, documenting the fix was complicated and expensive.

Lessons

The error in this instance went undetected because the template used by original counsel was old, from the early 1990s, when it was common for changes to board composition to be documented in the board minutes, in the articles, and in the bylaws, and the subsequent reviewers (the office manager and the new corporate counsel) were only accustomed to seeing board changes documented in the minutes and the bylaws, so they looked at the articles only for verification of the changes in capitalization and didn't look any farther.

This was a hard one. The original corporate counsel had a certain level of expertise in assisting start-ups. The office manager and the new corporate counsel both had expertise in start-up corporate governance, both reviewed the corporate governance documents, and both missed the change hidden in the articles. Perhaps this example best illustrates how even the smallest, unintended error in corporate governance documentation can have a far-reaching impact. If the error had been noted by the office manager or the replacement corporate counsel, there would still have been consequences because of the activities that had been transacted during the interim. This particular error would have had to have been caught at the time of the original transaction by original corporate counsel or the CEO in order to avoid the subsequent complications.

The lessons, then, must be:

- when using templates, look at the entire document;
- don't assume you know everything contained in the document;
- when doing a corporate governance review, look at each document as if you had never seen one like it before; and
- don't look only for information you expect to find.

Check and Double-Check

Robyn Shutak, NASPP

A mid-size semiconductor company offered a tax-qualified ESPP to its employees. Immediately following the close of the stock market on the day of purchase, the plan administrator looked up the company's stock price on Yahoo! Finance and used that price as the purchase price for the ESPP offering period in its stock plan system. The purchase was processed, and shares were distributed to all participant accounts.

Months later, an employee contacted the plan administrator. She had identified a difference between the company-referenced purchase price and various online resources, including Yahoo! Finance. The stock plan administrator investigated and found that the employee's discovery was accurate. Apparently Yahoo! Finance prices aren't always real time, and the price hadn't been updated when the administrator pulled it off the Internet. And, what's worse, the plan administrator had not documented how he arrived at the purchase price, so there was no backup documentation to support the original price.

The company had to reverse and reprocess the ESPP purchase, which meant that all interim activity also had to be reprocessed—backing out all employee terminations and withdrawals that occurred following the purchase, reversing any sales of the purchased ESPP stock and the

ESPP purchase itself, then re-entering the corrected purchase price, re-calculating the ESPP share distribution, re-entering post-purchase sales, and then, finally, re-entering all post-purchase terminations and withdrawals—plus communicating the mistake to employees, affected ex-employees, the transfer agent, and brokers.

Lessons

Any time an external source is used for primary data, the stock plan administrator should have a validation procedure in place as part of the company's SOX controls. Such procedures should include:

- Having a written policy that states what source(s) are to be used to obtain the primary data.
- Using multiple credible sources to obtain the data, such as NASDAQ.com *and* Morningstar (this is not an endorsement of any stock price reporting service, only a note that the service should be reputable).
- If the primary data is a stock price, then the plan should state how the stock price will be determined—opening, closing, or average stock price on the transaction date.
- Taking a screenshot or printing a PDF or hard copy of each primary-source display of the price, and indicating the time and date the information was obtained.
- Having a second person sign off on the use of the final number, with a written policy about what to do if the sources have conflicting primary data results.

Away Team to Scotty

Achaessa James, NCEO

The most complicated part of outsourcing or co-sourcing is, without question, communication; especially when the company uses more than one vendor to do different parts of the equity compensation work. For example, early-stage companies often keep their stock ledger and option ledger with outside corporate counsel. But corporate counsel only does legal work, and so another consultant is hired to do the option expensing. Sometimes the communication looks like the mess made by the Star Trek transporter when it combined the away team's molecular structure and forgot how to separate it properly.

My Australia-based client was an early-stage company, in business for about five years and on a strict budget. The stock and option ledger were maintained by corporate counsel on its software for "free." The company's HR director kept counsel up to date on terminations and new hires. Looking to economize, the company had negotiated a good subscription price with an accounting outsource service that duplicated the option ledger on a separate equity compensation SaaS platform to accomplish the equity compensation expensing. When the accounting service folded, the company negotiated a reduced-rate annual subscription with the second equity compensation SaaS platform vendor instead of paying a higher price to counsel's software provider for access to its expensing module. I was hired to update the expensing database every quarter and run the expense reports.

When the first quarter came, I asked the HR director for a payroll census to update the participant terminations, uploaded the new grants from counsel's database, and...the vested and forfeit numbers didn't match. Many emails later, we had reconciled counsel's database and the HR payroll census and then reconciled the expensing database.

When the second quarter came, the HR director sent me a payroll census to update the participant terminations, I uploaded the new grants from counsel's database, and, again, the vested and forfeit numbers didn't match. During this cycle, I noted that HR had reported some terminations late, after the prior quarter end, so we had to do a true-up from the prior quarter numbers...but counsel's database had not indicated that in any way, so it took a full reconciliation to figure out the cause of the differences. In addition, some previously terminated employees had been rehired, and the company had belatedly noted that the employees had actually stayed on the entire time as consultants during the "termination" period, so it had really been two change-in-status events instead of a termination and rehire, with the result that ISOs had converted to NSOs but continued vesting and were not forfeit. As before, many emails, several weeks, and a huge amount of billable hours later, we had reconciled counsel's database and the HR payroll census, and then reconciled the expensing database.

When the third quarter came, it was the fiscal year end and the company was in a big hurry to close the books. Again, my preliminary reconciliation showed that the historic records from the prior period had changed without explanation from counsel or HR. I knew that reconciling with counsel would take weeks—and I felt strongly that it was not my place to be policing whether counsel had reconciled the data with company HR. In the end, I consulted with my business partner, a CPA who specializes in equity accounting, and we decided it would be best to simply declare the counsel's database as the system of record, true up the expensing database to that official record, keep track of all of the changes made to do the true-up, and report it all back to the company's controller who was overseeing the entire process. I ran the recommendation by the controller, and she agreed that it was the most logical course of action.

I did the database true-up, detailed every little change that was made to conform it with counsel's data, ran the expense reports, figured out the true-ups, and had the CPA prepare the journal entries. Then we delivered the whole package to the client along with our significantly smaller invoices and were pleased to report no time spent in back and forth with counsel and HR.

Lessons

The lessons here are pretty simple—when using multiple databases, decide at the beginning:

- Which database will be the system of record.
- Whether the secondary database will be reconciled or will simply be trued up.
- A clear line of authority and responsibilities, including:
  - Who reconciles the primary database.
  - Who in the company communicates with which vendor.
  - Do the vendors communicate directly or only through the company liaison?

This situation still makes my stomach hurt when I think about it. Since the second quarter update, I have suggested to the company that it would be better, both economically and from a data integrity perspective, if it gave up the expensing database and simply contracted with counsel's software vendor for segregated access to the expensing module, but no decision has been reached. Our third quarter decision was not a perfect solution, but we are hoping that in the next quarter there will be no conflicts with counsel's database. I know that there is a high likelihood that it will not reconcile and that I will have to do a detailed true-up log again.

Checking It Twice

Mike Stevens, Alston & Bird LLP

A large private company issued equity awards on an annual basis. Lists of potential grantees were compiled by area managers based upon employee performance evaluations. The CEO would, in turn, evaluate the managers and executives and compile the master list before presenting the list to the compensation committee for approval. The list typically included over 100 employees.

The compensation committee reviewed the list, paying particular attention to the aggregate awards to be issued, both as a whole and at different employee levels. Little time was spent discussing individual grants at the lower employee levels. If the numbers were appropriate, the committee largely relied on management to identify the worthy employees.

Resolutions authorizing the awards were relatively standard, describing the material terms of the awards and the date of grant. Grantees were identified by attaching the list as an exhibit after the committee made any revisions it felt necessary or appropriate.

One year, several weeks after annual grants were approved and announced, an employee asked her manager why she hadn't received an award. She had received a stellar evaluation, and her manager had indicated that she would be recommended for a grant. The manager made some inquiries and discovered that, somewhere along the line, the employee's name had been left off of the list. The error was purely an oversight—everyone at her job level who received a top evaluation was to receive the same award. There is no question that management intended to propose the award and little risk that the committee would not have followed the proposal.

But her name wasn't on the list. Which meant that her intended grant wasn't part of the resolution. Which meant that her grant wasn't made.

After discussing various alternatives, management took the issue back to the board and circulated a consent action to approve the special grant to the employee.

Lessons

Board (or committee) approval is required under most plans and under most state corporate laws, with the exception of certain instances of limited authority delegated to officers. Accordingly, it is important that the board materials be complete and accurate.

If different categories of employees are receiving a certain number of awards (e.g., all VPs receive 100 options, all SVPs receive 150, and so on), then consider describing those grant categories in the resolutions, in addition to attaching a list. Such a description will help to describe the intent of the board in authorizing the awards.

Where an employee is simply left off of the list, and there is no broader description of awards and grantees in the resolutions, you cannot "fix" the error by substituting a corrected list in the board materials (that's granting without board authority), or by approving it later but granting it "as of" the original date (that's backdating). The best way to correct the problem is to own up to the mistake and seek board action. Most boards can act without a meeting by signing a unanimous written consent. Keep in mind, though, that the approval via consent generally is not effective until the last director signs the action. Accordingly, if a director is unreachable for some reason, the grant date will be delayed.

Alternatively, you could offer the employee a make-whole grant (i.e., a grant having the same value as the intended award, not just the same number of shares as the originally intended award) at a later date. This would be especially appropriate where you are granting stock options and the stock price has risen by the time the error is discovered.

Don't Assume...

Mark Miller, Deloitte Tax

Years ago, I had a client on the cutting edge of equity compensation granting restricted stock units (RSUs) for the first time to employees all over the world. It was important to the client to get this right, and the client went to great pains to implement controls and procedures at the U.S. level to understand country-specific tax withholding and reporting requirements. In addition, the client designed and implemented sophisticated systems to facilitate compliance with complex accounting rules.

When the RSUs began vesting, tax withholding was addressed by netting shares at the U.S. broker level and the cash equivalent of the shares withheld was remitted to local payrolls around the world, along with a summary of gains, for processing and remittance to the tax authorities.

Overall the process seemed to work well—the awards vested, the shares were released, the client's employees were happy.

On the backend, the taxes were sent to the global payrolls for processing as planned, with a view to local payrolls facilitating the remittance to the respective tax authorities and reporting in the employees' wage statements. As such, at the U.S. level, it was believed that the employer compliance obligations were met. However, at some point, the process broke down. In one country in particular (and unfortunately, the home of one of the larger subsidiaries), while e-mails and cash transfers had been sent, no one had spoken directly with the local payroll representatives to determine that they understood their critical role in the whole transaction. As it happened, the local payroll lead had not understood the file received. Unfortunately for everyone, rather than ask for clarification, the payroll lead chose to await further instructions which never came, and ultimately everyone forgot about the transaction and moved on. The foreign entity held the cash, nothing was paid over to the tax authorities, and nothing was reported in payroll.

Over a year passed and various RSU vestings occurred before the large (and increasing) cash balance in intercompany accounts was identified and questioned. At that point a review ensued, and the process issue was discovered. After hundreds of staff hours for the company and significant expense with outside counsel, a voluntary disclosure was initiated to contact the tax authorities to disclose the compliance issue and remit the proper taxes (with interest and penalties).

Had the local payroll acted timely, there would have been close to zero cost to them (they were simply passing through employee tax withholding). The subsidiary's failure to act cost the company cash and personnel resources.

Lessons

It may sound like a cliché, but don't forget to dot the "i's" and cross the "t's," and in the case of tax withholding, don't forget that the corporate obligation is not fulfilled until the tax authorities receive their money and the payroll reporting is operated appropriately.

While the company had diligently mapped out a robust methodology for addressing the employer compliance obligations at the U.S. level, the local business partners were not directly engaged and there were miscommunications based on written communications. A simple phone call to confirm understanding could have alleviated most if not all of the effort. Key lesson: if you don't hear back, don't assume that all is well. Don't be afraid to pick up the phone and confirm that what you think should be happening overseas, actually is transpiring.

Chapter 3

Culture and Cultivation

The plan is designed and approved. The policies and procedures are in place for proper administration. Next comes deciding how much equity to give out, to whom, in what forms, and under what circumstances. Again, cookie-cutter approaches seldom work the way the experts selling them say they will.

Another important consideration is having a basic understanding of how the awards are going to affect your employees. Will the gain on an incentive stock option exercise require your employee to pay alternative minimum tax? If so, perhaps you might consider granting non-qualified stock options. Will equity compensation income affect your employee's ability to take out student loans for her college-age child? How will the policies and procedures you've put into place affect your employees? Are you comfortably able to apply all of those policies and procedures in a consistent manner across the board, without exception? I ask because even though your termination policy is to not provide notice to departing employees about the post-termination exercise period for their vested shares, will you be comfortable with treating the widow of one of your loyal employees the same when her husband passes away unexpectedly?

The idea at this stage is to take a good look at what you've built and visualize how it will play out in the lives of the people who make up your company.

But the Surveys Said...

Corey Rosen, National Center for Employee Ownership

A well-established company wanted to figure out how much equity to give to key people. So it got some survey data and decided to pay just above the median. If everyone else was doing it, shouldn't they? They looked at two things: the percentage of the company each position received and the value of the awards (the latter was harder to get good data on, however). It seemed like a sensible approach, but I told them it had some real limits.

Lessons

At the NCEO, we do compensation surveys, so we know a lot about how this sausage is made. Compensation surveys suffer multiple selection bias problems:

- *The less well you are doing, the less likely you are to respond.* There is a natural tendency, even in an anonymous survey, not to want to hang out your dirty laundry. Many surveys also charge a fee to participate (you get the results in return), making this tendency even more marked. So your comparison sample will err on the high side of compensation.
- *Many surveys are of compensation consultant clients.* These groups are self-selecting in a variety of ways, not the least of which is that they are able to pay a compensation consultant. The consultants may also have already advised them on their favorite approaches to compensation.
- *Many surveys have limited sample size, especially for relevant comparison groups.* The margin of error in survey results is very large in samples under 100 or so (that's not a magic line, of course; the more the better). Say a survey has 1,000 respondents from all over the country and in various industries. If you really want an apt comparison, you want to look at a fairly narrowly defined set of companies in similar businesses in places with similar costs of living. Even with 1,000 overall respondents, this may mean your relevant sample is only 10 or 20, and at that number, the results can be wildly off.
- *Job titles among respondents may not match.* Two people may have the same title but very different responsibilities. This is especially true for technology companies.

If you do use surveys, consider how the mean (average) and median (the point at which half the companies are larger and half smaller) differ. Bill Gates and any small African country have a reasonable mean income, but the median is another story. If the survey sample is skewed (usually by a few executives with a lot of compensation), the median may be better. But the sample could also have a bunch of unrepresentative companies in one range, making the mean better. You can get a better sense of this from a calculation called the standard deviation. A simple explanation of this is that it measures the range around the mean in which two-third of the sample falls. If it is very large, the mean is not very useful.

Also think about whether your real comparison is by job, not industry. A software engineer or CFO can work for all kinds of companies, for instance. Also, don't cherry-pick particular pieces of compensation. If you find that CFOs get a certain size reward in equity, that does not mean yours should as well. You have to consider what other compensation there is, as well as what non-financial benefits (work flexibility, vacation, meaningful work, etc.) are provided. Unfortunately, few surveys give you the whole picture, and almost none report on company contributions to qualified benefit plans, such as 401(k) programs.

Given all these issues, it makes sense to use surveys not to set a specific target but as a reality check setting broad parameters, such as aiming at between the 25th and 75th percentiles. To set compensation, start instead with internal equity. How much more do Joe and Mary contribute to the company than Sam and Veronica? Their compensation should be aligned roughly with that relative contribution or you are paying some people too much and some too little (unless getting someone for that job simply requires an otherwise inequitable reward).

Let's Give Out 10%, Most of It Up-Front. It's What I Hear Most Companies Do

Corey Rosen, National Center for Employee Ownership

I can't count the number of times I have had this conversation. A company CEO calls and says he or she would like to share equity with employees. "What were you thinking of doing?" I ask, suspecting the answer. Most say "we want to give out about 10% of the equity, most of it now, to our current people, but keeping some for later." "And why do you want to do that?" I ask innocently. "Well," they say, "it's what I was told other people do."

Many years ago I heard the well-known business author Tom Peters ask what company wants as its motto "we were like everyone else"? So just because others do it, does not mean it makes sense for your company. In fact, it can create two big problems:

- *10% of your company is not worth the same as 10% of another company.* As I noted in another case, employees don't really care so much about what percentage of the company they own, and especially don't care about what aggregate percentage of shares they all own. They care about what it is worth. So would you rather have 0.5% of a new start-up with minimal investment and uncertain prospects or 0.5% of a third-year company with a product, investors, a product, and (gasp) profits?
- *If you give most of it away now, what happens if you grow?* Now you are bringing on new people, often at levels of similar or even greater responsibility, but you have little equity left to give them. No issue rankles people more at work than perceived unfairness in compensation, so this is a recipe for lots of problems.

Lessons

When deciding how much to give out, think about what it's worth to you and the employees, not just the percentage of the company it represents. And don't give away too much to start if you can avoid it. Instead, think about equity awards as you might think about bonuses. You give bonuses, usually annually, based on individual, group, or company performance, or some combination. Why not do the same with equity? Say your target growth for the year is 15% and you hit it. Then you might be willing to share some percentage of the added value that has created with eligible employees. If you hit a stretch goal, you might share even a bigger percentage. You can do that every year. By setting these targets, you might end up giving away a bigger percentage of the company than 10% or some other fixed number, but only because your company did well enough so that you own a smaller piece of a bigger company. If you don't meet the targets, then you own a bigger piece of a smaller one because you don't give anything away. Employees see a target they can shoot for, which is motivating in itself. They see that they can always get more, and they get rewarded regularly, rather than a file-and-forget-it grant on hire.

You still want to set some parameters—maybe you never want to give up more than 20%, for instance, but this greater flexibility should work to everyone's advantage.

It's Just the Key People Who Should Get Equity, Right?

Corey Rosen, National Center for Employee Ownership

It's the mantra of most compensation consultants. Just the key contributors should get equity. That is what Pareto Systems thought, too. "After all," the CEO thought, "80% of the results come from 20% of the people, and besides, only a few of the 20% really have much direct input into how the stock does. Besides, people at lower levels have no line of sight to stock prices, and they know their individual efforts can't matter much anyway."

Pareto had a chance to put this theory into practice when it bought a company where everyone was an owner, receptionist on up. "We loved the company. It had a fantastic culture, and we wanted that to be part of us," the CEO told me. "But after a year or so, they were just ordinary again. We paid them well, but absent that equity, things just really changed."

Lessons

Just because something makes intuitive sense does not mean it is correct. Intuitively, it might seem that only "key" people will care about stock awards or deserve them. Intuitively, it might seem if I am one of 500 or 5,000 or 50,000 people, I will be happy to be a "free rider" on the efforts of others. But an equally intuitive argument can be made that if everyone is an owner, and is treated like an owner, then everyone will all be more interested in contributing ideas, saving money, and working more cooperatively with other people. Like countless CEOs say, people are a company's most important asset. They say that, but then they turn around and compensate just a few people as the company's most important asset.

Intuition, however, should not rule such an important decision when we have ample data on what actually does work. According to Joseph Blasi and Douglas Kruse of Rutgers, who have studied this issue for over two decades, the evidence is clear that broad-based equity plans increase shareholder return more than narrowly focused ones. You can find details on all the research on the NCEO Web site at www.nceo.org, in the articles and research section.

Their research, and that of countless others, has shown that people's motivation at work is a lot more complicated than "if I do this, I will get that amount of money." The expectations of their peers, how challenging a job is, their sense of autonomy at work, whether they perceive they are being treated fairly, and other largely non-economic factors all matter more than simple economic calculations of benefit maximization. Economan lives in textbooks; he does not work for you. While people will rarely make a calculation that if they make this much more effort, that will have this much more impact on their stock price, being granted equity tells them the company values them, gives them an incentive to stay, and provides a great teaching opportunity for the company to show how collective employee efforts affect the bottom line.

Venture capitalists seemed to have figured this out. Eighty-five percent of venture-backed companies give equity to most employees; about 75% give it to everyone. You may have a really great CEO and a terrific product, but a surly receptionist will prevent a customer from buying it. Your employees may have a lot of good ideas about ways to cut waste, satisfy customers, generate new products, save energy, and on and on, but if they feel like second-class citizens, they won't be engaged enough to share them (and besides, no one will likely ask; after all, only 20% of the employees really matter, if that). Sharing equity broadly is simply a good investment.

But what about the 80-20 rule? It's kind of a law of nature, right? It turns out that the 80-20 rule is a myth, not a law. Back in the late 19th century, Italian economist Wilfredo Pareto (our company's namesake) observed that 80% of the land was owned by 20% of the people. In the 1940s, management consultant Kenneth Juran argued that the 80-20 rule must apply to management in general, concluding that there were the "vital few and the trivial many." That seemed a bit harsh, so he later revised it to the "vital few and the useful many." Unfortunately for Juran, there is not, as far as I can tell, a single study that actually empirically confirms this "rule."

In fact, it is highly corrosive idea. First, everyone who writes and reads about it, I'd wager, believes he or she is in the 20%, so it sounds good to them. In fact, numerous studies have demonstrated the "Lake Wobegon" effect in which large majorities of people believe they are above or well-above average on just about every dimension they are asked about. So an 80-20 practice leaves most people annoyed. Second, if you treat people as if they don't matter that much, you may well end up with an organization where they don't. So your brilliance in following the 80-20 rules is self-fulfilling. Third, the 80-20 rule creates too much competition between people for scarce rewards, thus discouraging teamwork. Why would I want to help my colleague or my boss shine so he or she can get the great rewards while I languish in the mediocre 80%? Fourth, the 80-20 rule encourages turnover. If I see I am not going to be in top 20%, and I can find some other employer who'll treat me better, I'm out of here. Even for the just "useful" 80%, high turnover is a very costly problem.

So next time someone invokes the 80-20 rule, ask them for a study that actually shows it.

All Shares Are Not Created Equal

Corey Rosen, National Center for Employee Ownership

All shares are not created equal, even if they do have certain inalienable rights endowed by their creators (at least not alienable without a contractual change).

I have received more than one call from an entrepreneur whose plan is to give all employees a certain number of equity awards, whether they join this year or another year. Different levels of employees will get different amounts, but everyone at the same level gets the same. To the entrepreneurs, this seemed fair—everyone with the same responsibilities got the same amount.

It usually takes a while for people to understand that the same number of awards does not have the same value if granted at different times. An option granted at $10 does not have the same value as one granted at $15. If the stock doubles after the award, the $15 option yields

50% more in returns. The same line of reasoning applies to all kinds of equity awards. This seems pretty obvious, but it must not be. Consider, for instance, how many public companies some years ago gave everyone 100 options in different years.

To take a more sophisticated problem, consider how many experts waxed poetic about how restricted stock or stock-settled stock appreciation rights (SSARs) are less dilutive than stock options. In the same simplistic way the entrepreneurs thought about the problem, this is true. If we have one million shares and give options on 100,000 of them, we have a nominal 10% dilution. If we give restricted stock, we might commonly only have to give out one-third as many shares, and SSARs could result in even fewer shares.

But if we have defined the grants in advance to provide the equivalent present value of the awards regardless of their form, then the economic dilution (as opposed to the dilution in the number of shares) is by definition the same. As a shareholder, one approach means I own a smaller piece of a bigger pie (options) and the other (restricted stock, for instance) means I have a bigger piece of a smaller pie. That's because restricted stock has value even if the share price goes down (that is why you can give out fewer shares). The only conceivable reason I or anyone else should care about dilution in terms of the number of shares is dilution of control, and that is just not a real issue given the percentage of a company likely to end up in shares employees acquire and hold from exercising an option. Yet advisors commonly urged companies to do this to reduce dilution, presumably because they thought investors were too dense to go beyond the nominal dilution awards created.

Lessons

The lesson here is simple. When you think about equity awards, think about the present value of the award, not the number. The first thing employees do when they get an award is try to figure out what it is worth, not what number of shares they have or what percentage of the company they have. Neither, in itself, buys you that new car or a down payment on a house.

I Gave Them Equity, but They Thought It Was Worth a Lot Less Than I Did

Corey Rosen, National Center for Employee Ownership

Oscar Crouch had a great idea for a start-up. CookieMonster.com would be an online source for small bakeries. Companies would be lured online by user groups sharing recipes, marketing strategies, customer service tips, design ideas, and more. The company would make money by selling specialized software for inventory management, accounting, tax reporting, payroll management, and more.

To lure employees with the needed skills, Oscar offered everyone nonqualified stock options (NSOs). The options were granted at fair market value. The terms were these:

- Vesting: 33.3% per year.
- Term: The options could be exercised for up to eight years once fully vested.
- Liquidity: The employees could only sell the shares they had exercised on a liquidity event, defined as an initial public offering or a change of control transaction.

Oscar gave NSOs that, on a fully diluted basis, were worth 10% of the total equity. He planned to make another 10% available for additional grants over the next three years. So, in his mind, his was giving up 20% of the company, which he figured conservatively would be worth at least $1 million in three years.

His employees thought otherwise. Ernie, a software programmer, told Oscar he figured his grant of 1,000 NSOs at a face value of $100 per share was worth about $500. Bert, his CFO, was savvier. He thought his grant of 5,000 NSOs at that price was worth about $5,000. Oscar objected. "My accountant, Grover Ledger, put a charge of one-third the face value of the NSOs on my income statement as a compensation cost. You guys are valuing these way too low!"

Oscar was suffering an asymmetry problem. The awards imposed real pain on him, but employees foresaw much less real gain. What was going on?

Lessons

Oscar's problem is a common one. In recent years, economists have come to a much better understanding of how people think about money. People tend to undervalue the actual value of equity awards (the value Grover carefully calculated using traditional economic analysis) based on four factors:

1. *Risk:* People tend to overvalue the importance of risk. If the chance of getting an award is, say, actually 50%, employees might think of that as more likely a 25% chance.
2. *Time:* People have an excessive preference for immediate rewards. For instance, studies show that most people would prefer $5 today to $10 next week. This undervaluing of the time value of money means that if an option won't be exercisable or the shares sellable for several years, an accountant might say they are worth "x," but employees will see it as some fraction of x.
3. *Loss versus gain:* People value a dollar of loss much more than a dollar of gain. If you ask people who have lost $50 if they want a double or nothing bet, most say yes. If they have made $50, most will turn down a double or nothing debt. Similarly, people tend to be more reluctant to sell a losing stock than a winning stock that has gained as much.
4. *People underestimate how long they will stay at a job:* You may have had this experience yourself. You take a new job and expect to be there for a year or a few years at most, then end up being there for much longer. That's a typical experience for a lot of people. The problem this creates for options is that people may believe (1) they will never vest and/or (2) if they do, they won't be there to sell the shares.

With an option, if you have to pay to exercise, and then pay tax, you have an immediate loss with only a seemingly risky chance of it paying off, and then not for some time. So what they seem to be worth to the seller and what they seem to be worth to employees is very different.

So what could Oscar do? One possibility is Oscar can convince people that a liquidity event is highly likely in a few years. An IPO is, realistically, unlikely—very few companies that think they can do an

IPO really can. Building the company for sale is more realistic. If this is also uncertain, Oscar could consider a few alternatives:

- *Provide stock-settled stock appreciation rights instead.* A stock appreciation right (SAR) provides the right to the increase in the value of shares over a period of time, subject to vesting rules, just like a stock option. An SAR can be settled in cash or stock, however. Settling in cash (paying for the difference between the grant and exercise price) doesn't solve Oscar's problem. If he had the cash, he could also just buy back the shares employees bought from options exercises. Instead, he can give employees the award in shares. Employees would still have to pay taxes, but the pain would be less than exercising an option, which also requires buying the shares. If the company has the cash, it could provide a bonus to help employees pay part or all of the taxes.
- *Provide an internal market for shares.* If employees do have options and end up with shares, Oscar could have the company buy them back if it has the cash and/or set up an informal exchange where people can let it be known they have shares to sell that other employees or, conceivably, investors might buy.
- *Make the awards exercisable only on a liquidity event.* If all else fails, the awards could be exercisable only if there is a sale or IPO. That way, employees have no current pain from exercising an option to get shares they cannot yet sell. It does, however, make the incentive value of the award less real, especially if the event seems uncertain or years away.

Four and Twenty Blackbirds

Bruce Brumberg, myStockOptions.com

Q. My husband passed away two summers ago. I was not aware, and his company did not notify me, that he had stock options which were about to expire at the beginning of this year. Even if I had been aware, I did not have exercise rights, as his will was in probate and I was not approved as executrix until this summer. His company would not tell me any detailed information because I did not have a letter of testamentary. Is there any way to retrieve the lost money on the expired options?

A. We are sorry to hear about your husband. Companies are usually very strict about their post-termination exercise rules, even in a situation involving death. If they were to allow exercises after the deadline (e.g., beyond 90 days after standard job termination or beyond 12 months after death), they would need to do this for everyone, and the extension might be considered a modification of the stock grant.

Sometimes options continue to vest after death. It's not clear from your question whether these options are expiring at end of the full term, or are expiring because they reached the end of the post-termination exercise period. The delay in giving you the power to exercise them does not extend this period, unless the stock plan says otherwise. Some companies allow appointing beneficiaries for stock grants, a move that would avoid probate.

Otherwise, the stock grant will pass through probate under the terms of any will or state laws of descent. The post-termination exercise period does not wait to start until an administrator is appointed or the beneficiary receives notice. Even when a specific beneficiary is designated, the options, stock, and/or stock appreciation rights are still included in the estate's value for tax purposes.

Lessons

This Q&A emphasizes the need for the company to have a written policy and consistent application of the policy, but it also raises the question of fairness and the utility of transparency. In this case, the company appears to have a policy that when an employee dies no notification is provided to the decedent's beneficiary or estate about the status of unexercised equity compensation awards. Under that policy, the amount of time to stabilize the estate exceeded the amount of time allowed for post-termination exercise of the vested awards, and the awards were forfeit.

Is that fair? Should the company have made an effort to notify the estate? There are no right or wrong answers here, just questions that a company must consider when establishing policies and consistently executing them.

It's also something to consider that, while the policy at this company relieved the company from the burden of having to contact the estate of every deceased employee (really, how many employees die each year and how much time would it take to notify their estates?), if the awards were of a significant monetary value it would not be unheard of for an estate representative to complain to an attorney and the attorney press a claim against the company—knowing that the claim was perhaps not supported by law, but counting on the company to settle the case for its "nuisance value" rather than incur the costs of litigating or arbitrating the case.

So which would better serve the company and its shareholders—a policy of transparency that requires a bit more staff time on the front end, or a policy that requires no response on the front end but considerable more time and money when, as they say, the crows come home to roost?

The Hip Bone's Connected to the Thigh Bone...

Bruce Brumberg, myStockOptions.com

Q. To qualify for federal college financial aid for my daughter, including loans, I need to complete and submit the Free Application for Federal Student Aid (FAFSA) to the U.S. Department of Education annually. This form determines our eligibility for federal financial aid as well as scholarships, grants, and other aid opportunities. I have stock options that can be exercised. Do I need to list these on the FAFSA form? At what value?

A. As long as the student is considered a dependent of the parent for financial aid purposes, the parent does have to report the stock options on line 82 of the FAFSA (http://www.fafsa.ed.gov). This line states: "As of today, what is the net worth of your parents' investments, including real estate (not your parents' home)? Net worth means current value minus debt." The definition of "investments" includes "stock options" and "other securities" but provides little guidance on whether this includes employee stock options and at what value.

From informal discussions with the Department of Education that we have heard about, we believe the value that should be reported is the net value (after fees, commissions, taxes, etc.) of all types of vested stock options as if they were sold at market value on the day the form is completed. The same rules apply for employee stock purchase plans.

Lessons

The decision to make employee ownership part of your corporate culture is an admirable one that often also has a positive impact on the company's bottom line. But how will it affect your employees? This is another example that illustrates just how complicated equity compensation can be, how it can have an effect on unexpected areas of an award recipient's financial life, and how important it is to have expert resources available to your employees via your plan administrator. A summary of this Q&A would be a perfect addition to an online FAQ.

Option Income and Social Security

Bruce Brumberg, myStockOptions.com

Here is a last example of how equity compensation can have surprise consequences to an employee if the payroll department doesn't properly code the income from an option exercise.

Q. I am 62 years old and am receiving Social Security. I have stock options from my employer that were issued prior to my retirement. When I exercise my NSOs, I understand that a W-2 will be issued and the gain will be taxed as ordinary income. Yet the Social Security Web site (www.ssa.gov) indicates that investments and investment income are not income to be considered against the Social Security annual earnings limit. Therefore, when I exercise my options, what will the impact be on the annual earnings limit?

A. Income from the exercise of employee stock options is not investment income: it is compensation income. But since you received the options before retirement, and since the income is attributable to services rendered before retirement, it should not have an impact on the excess-earnings test. Ask your employer to use the proper code on your Form W-2 so that the Social Security Administration knows what has occurred.

Lessons

The important takeaway from this Q&A is that there are many stakeholders in a company who must understand how equity compensation should be treated by each particular department. Having a properly qualified stock plan administrator (read that as CEP) will help to keep all the bases covered, but the stakeholders in other departments must have a clear understanding that equity compensation income is treated differently and know to ask for clarification when personal knowledge is not sufficient.

ISO Hidden Tax Costs

Bruce Brumberg, myStockOptions.com

One of my pet peeves about incentive stock options is the little-discussed potential for triggering the alternative minimum tax, especially ISOs exercised by employees in non-public companies that cannot be sold in a disqualifying disposition at year-end to avoid triggering the AMT. The Q&A below illustrates various useful ISO/AMT scenarios.

Q. I know that if I have a huge income hit through an NSO exercise I might have to pay estimated taxes. What about an ISO exercise in which I plan to hold the stock after exercise? I will have a gain of about $200,000, which almost certainly will trigger AMT. Do I need to pay estimated taxes on ISOs when the AMT I owe is much greater than my current salary withholding?

A. Tax law imposes a penalty on taxpayers who do not pay "enough" tax during the year, either through withholding or through estimated tax payments. The tax that has to be paid includes any AMT attributable to the exercise of ISOs. In order to avoid this penalty, which is actually a nondeductible interest charge (the current rate is 8%), the law provides a number of safe harbors. The most common ones are:

1. Pay 90% of the current year's tax liability ratably throughout the year (withholding is automatically treated as paid ratably; estimated tax payments are credited when actually paid). This method requires you to estimate what your liability will ultimately be for the current year.
2. Pay an amount equal to 100% of the prior year's tax liability (including AMT) ratably throughout the year (withholding is automatically treated as paid ratably; estimated tax payments are credited when actually paid). If your Adjusted Gross Income for the prior year was more than $150,000, the percentage of the prior year's tax you must pay is greater: 110% in 2001, 112% in 2002, and 110% in 2003 and later. This method is useful if you have a substantially higher tax liability during the current year, since your required payments are limited and based on the prior year's liability. It is not helpful when your liability is expected to go down.
3. Pay 90% annually of an amount calculated each period based on your taxable items (including AMT items) for that period. For example, if your taxable income in March is $30,000, you calculate the tax on $120,000 of taxable income ($30,000 x 4), divide the result by 4, and multiply it by 90%. You then determine how much tax had been withheld and pay the difference as an estimated tax payment. This method works best when income is earned unequally throughout the year.

To the extent that payments you make throughout the year are short of one of these safe harbors, the penalty will apply.

Lessons

This is another example that illustrates just how complicated equity compensation can be, how there can be multiple outcomes from a single contemplated transaction, and how important it is to instruct your employees to consult with their tax professionals prior to making any exercise transactions to best understand the effect of the transaction on their personal situations.

ISO, AMT, and a Falling Stock Price

Bruce Brumberg, myStockOptions.com

Here is another circumstance that falls under the question of whether transparency is important in a company's notification policy.

Q. Our company grants ISOs that vest and become exercisable on the same day. They are not early exercise ISOs subject to repurchase by the company. I exercised 2,000 ISOs with a $5 exercise price in February when the stock was at $40. The stock crashed and is now at $4. The $70,000 spread at exercise ($35 x 2,000 shares) is part of my calculation for alternative minimum tax (AMT). It looks like my AMT liability will exceed my regular tax liability by approximately $18,000. Can I now sell the stock at $4 and negate the $70,000 added back for AMT purposes?

A. Yes, as long as you sell the shares on or before December 31, 2000. By selling the shares that you acquired from the exercise of an ISO in the same calendar year as the exercise, you effectively eliminate the AMT adjustment.

Generally, the spread at exercise of an ISO (difference between the fair market value on date of exercise and the exercise price) is a positive adjustment (here, $70,000) for AMT purposes. Federal tax law required you to pay the greater of your regular tax liability or your AMT liability. However, because you exercised the option in February 2000 and you are selling the shares in 2000, you will eliminate the adverse AMT effects of the ISOs.

In addition to the AMT consequences, your sale of the shares will have regular tax consequences. Ordinarily, when you sell ISOs before satisfying the required federal tax holding periods for incentive stock options (two years from the date of grant of the option; one year from the date of exercise of the option), you would be required to report income equal to the lesser of (1) the spread at exercise, or (2) the excess of the sales price over the exercise price. In your case, however, this amount is zero.

Also, since you will be selling at less than your exercise price, you have a short-term capital loss of $1 per share or $2000. You offset this short-term capital loss against any capital gains for 2000 or, if none, against ordinary income (e.g., your salary) earned in 2000. Federal tax laws allow up to $3,000 of short-term capital losses to be used in this manner. Any excess carries over to the next tax year.

Lessons

So, again, there is no right or wrong answer, only the question—will your company make this information available to employees who have exercised ISOs in a year that turned out to have a falling stock price? And, if so, how will you communicate that information to them?

And a slightly different question to non-public companies—do you advise your employees of the potential AMT consequences of exercising ISOs, especially since there is no way for them to later sell the stock to avoid AMT? And, if so, how do you communicate that information to them?

Chapter 4

Communication and Education

There are three audiences to plan for when you're budgeting for, designing, and implementing your roadmap for communication and education on equity compensation. Only one is obvious—employees. It's important that employees have enough information to understand the value of the awards they've received and make intelligent decisions for their financial futures. Sometimes this means that one-to-one Q&A is appropriate. Sometimes a lunch-and-learn program is useful. Sometimes doing a company-wide event is appropriate. Sometimes making an online resource available is enough. Sometimes it simply means that you tell them to go see their own financial and tax professionals. Usually it means a combination of several methods.

The other two audiences aren't quite so top of mind, but they're even more important. First, you have to select an administrator who has the experience and education necessary to get the job done. I'll be up front about this—my personal and professional opinion is that if the person is not a Certified Equity Professional through the CEP Institute, then she is not fully qualified, and details are likely to slip through the cracks. There are other programs available that teach the basics, but to have a professional who knows enough to keep the company and the plan in compliance is the most important qualification, and that level of training is currently only available from the CEP Institute. Having said that, qualified equity compensation professionals make expert-level salaries, and not every company has the budget to staff such a high-level position, especially start-ups and early-stage ventures. In that case, just make sure that, whether you use a service provider or an individual consultant, the person in charge of your equity compensation database is a CEP.

And that person, the qualified professional administrator, will need to have superior communication skills to coordinate with the third key audience—internal stakeholders. Equity compensation touches every aspect of a company's business, including legal, tax, finance, HR, payroll, board of directors, executive team, and even down to line managers who have staff who receive awards. The equity compensation administrator needs to be able to effectively communicate with and educate stakeholders from each of these groups to coordinate periodic and project-specific activities. If the administrator can do this, the company's plan will stay in compliance, and the company will be more likely to meet its business goals for equity compensation.

Enough said. Here are some examples of failures in this area.

The Angry Millionaire

Dan Walter, Performensation Consulting

My coworker was crying. I worked with an outsourcing firm and she was on the phone getting yelled at by a plan participant. I took over the call and asked the participant to explain the issue.

"She just told me that I owe the government more than $4 million in taxes! There is no way I am going to pay that. It's stupid!"

I quickly looked up the participant's information and said, "Sir, I notice that you're an engineer. You probably make about $80,000 a year. As a result of the merger your company just went through, all of your option vesting has accelerated. Your options have a value of more than $12 million. Your taxes can be handled during the exercise transaction, and you will get a check for more than $8 million once your taxes are paid. That's about 100 times your annual pay. You are now a millionaire several times over...congratulations."

There was about three seconds of silence, and then, "I AM SO SORRY, can you hand the phone back to the other person so I can apologize in person?"

Lessons

In the equity compensation world, life-changing events usually carry life-changing taxes. Communicating those changes in context is a good idea. In this example, the first service provider explained only the taxes that resulted from the participant's exercise but failed to explain the reason for those taxes and that they could be deducted from his much larger gain.

Whether your option plan is administered in-house or outsourced, it's important that participant-facing service representatives have good communications skills. Teaching them to calculate the taxes on a transaction is useful, but teaching them to understand how that information may affect a participant and then communicate it in a way the participant can understand it is essential.

The Ecstatic Millionaire

Dan Walter, Performensation Consulting

It was 1996. "Stock options" was still not a household word. I was helping cover customer service phone lines and received a call from a very pleasant man who explained that he worked as a scientist for a company that had gone public a year earlier. He really didn't understand how everything worked, but his wife wanted to purchase a new car. Someone in human resources had told him to call us about the options he received pre-IPO. He thought there might be enough money to put a good down payment on something nice for his wife. It was their 25th anniversary and he wanted to make it special.

I looked up his information and told him that he should be able to buy a great car. I informed him that he currently had $1,284,000 in exercisable stock options. He asked me to repeat the number. When I did, he responded, "My wife will be happy," and hung up on me. About an hour a later he called me back and apologized for hanging up. He had never imagined that the options could have a value of even as much as his annual income, much less over a million dollars.

Lessons

The missing piece in this example is participant education. When a company takes an action that significantly affects the value of its employees' equity compensation awards, like an acquisition, merger, IPO, or other change-in-control event, educating the employees about those effects should be a key element in completing the corporate transaction.

This story had a very happy outcome—the employee found out he was a million dollars richer and could buy his wife a nice car. But what might have happened if the stock had gone way up and then lost all value in the year between the corporate transaction and the participant's call? If the company had provided basic education to employee participants, the obligation to keep on top of award values would sit squarely on the participants. On the other hand, if the company had not educated its employees, there would at best be some very disgruntled employees and at worst be some who decided to litigate the issue.

So remember, when allocating resources for a corporate transaction, employee education costs significantly less than legal fees.

What We Have Here Is a Failure to Communicate

Robyn Shutak, NASPP

Company GHI had a qualified employee stock purchase plan in place, and the stock administration department had been successfully managing the offerings for several years. The stock administration department was responsible for communicating ESPP open enrollment information to employees, collecting new enrollment/change forms and delivering this information to payroll. Payroll was responsible for processing payroll deductions every pay period throughout the offering period.

On a Monday at the start of a new offering period, the new ESPP specialist held the scheduled employee education Webinar, confirmed that all employees had been given enrollment forms in the morning mail run, and provided instruction on completing the forms to folks who called him. On Friday he counted the stack of enrollment and change forms he'd received through interoffice mail that week and noticed that he had about half the number he expected. Then he realized it was the Friday before a Monday holiday, and many employees had taken Friday off to make it an extra-long weekend. He decided to wait until the following week to turn in the enrollment forms so he could follow up with the unaccounted-for employees first.

On Tuesday following the holiday the ESPP specialist collected the remaining enrollment forms and presented them to payroll for processing. Imagine his surprise when the payroll supervisor informed him that payroll had been processed on Friday because of the Monday holiday and the ESPP payroll deductions would not be processed for the first pay period of the new offering. Imagine the dismay of the stock option department supervisor when she had to send out a communication to the participating employees explaining the mistake, explaining the various options they had for correcting the problem, and then ensuring that each and every instance was handled before the next payroll cutoff date the following week.

Lessons

As administrators, when we think about communication we often focus on employee participants. Do they understand the technical aspects of the awards? Do they know how to fill out their forms? Do they know the offering periods? This example is a good reminder that communication among departments can spoil even the best employee communication efforts. Here are some steps that could have been taken to avoid this ugly surprise:

- The payroll department provides the stock administration department with a copy of the payroll cutoff calendar at the beginning of every year or quarter.
- The stock administration department checks the payroll cutoff calendar at the beginning of every week to ensure timely submission of ESPP enrollment and change forms.
- The ESPP specialist calls the payroll department on the first day of the new offering period as a courtesy to remind them of the new activity period.
- The payroll processor calls the ESPP specialist the day before payroll cutoff as a courtesy as a reminder of the submission deadline.
- Department managers should meet regularly with their team to be sure critical deadlines are being met.

Better yet, implement online ESPP enrollment to do away with manual processes that invite these kinds of oversight.

It's a Surprise! But Not the Party Kind

Jennifer George, Orrick, Herrington & Sutcliffe LLP

"On the fly" when used in an automotive context refers to the ability to change from two-wheel drive to four-wheel drive while the car is in gear and moving. When used in the context of ice hockey, it means that player changes are made while play is still ongoing, with exiting players leaping over the boards and replacement players shooting onto the ice as quickly as possible to avoid wasting time in the exchange and to ensure that fresh players are on the ice as often as possible. A similar concept, hot swapping, refers to on-the-fly replacement of computer hardware.[1]

When used in the context of equity compensation, the image is closer to a fully suited ice hockey player changing the tire on a four-wheel drive SUV while the auto is in gear and moving. Read on, and you'll see what I mean.

I can't tell you how many times companies focus all their equity compensation planning and rollout efforts on the U.S. employee population and neglect to think about their non-U.S. population or simply put this analysis off until the plan/ program is about to be rolled out. Here are some of the on-the-fly projects I've had to work on in the past decade:

Stock option exchanges. A number of these have crossed my desk since the economic downturn, and several times I've received calls about rolling out an option exchange program "next week" and the client needs help with the non-U.S. tax and legal issues and the tender offer disclosures. Even in the U.S., option exchanges have distinct steps:

1. The board approves the offer.
2. Counsel prepares tender offer documentation.
3. HR distributes the tender offer to all option holders.
4. Option holders must either accept or reject the tender offer.
5. HR gathers the tender offer responses and transmits them to equity administration.
6. The equity administration platform is updated with the exchange:

---

1. "On the Fly," *Wikipedia,* http://en.wikipedia.org/wiki/On_the_fly.

- — Expense reports are run for the day immediately preceding the exchange date.
- — The exchange is processed on the options. This can be as easy as a one-step exchange, or as complicated as a cancel and reissue, depending upon the software.
- — Option pricing model factors are updated.
- — Expense reports are run for the day immediately after the exchange date.
- — Journal entries are created for the incremental difference in the equity compensation expense.

7. Counsel prepares new award documents, or old documents get a notice of amendment.
8. HR distributes the award modification documents to the affected option holders.

Now imagine those same steps, but add on the steps required for investigating foreign securities laws and tax regulations, and then include the extra complication that many foreign jurisdictions have extremely restrictive privacy laws that do not allow the transfer of employee personal data (not even the person's name) even between a parent and its subsidiary company without express written permission of each and every employee; and even if that written permission is in place for the parent company, it does not extend to any outsource service providers that may be used by the company. This is definitely not conducive to a "next week" timeline.

ESPPecially special. Then there are my clients who want to roll out an ESPP in three weeks and want to offer it in as many countries as possible. Or those who want to roll out any type of equity compensation program in China in three weeks. Apart from the usual concerns about foreign securities laws and tax laws, any program in a foreign country that will involve the exchange of currency has to meet that country's treasury regulations on currency control, and that entails establishing foreign banking relationships with a government-approved bank, forms and legal filings with government offices; often the country will require that the signatory to the filings be an in-country citizen. In China, compliance with the S.A.F.E. requirements is considered lightning fast if the process is completed in six months, as it consists of approvals at federal, provincial, and municipal levels.

Lessons

The lesson here is to keep your intentions in perspective. I'm not going to say that these timelines are impossible to work within, but they're not ideal and generally result in the disappointing news that we may not be able to offer all these programs in all desired countries on your preferred timeline, as we may not have enough time to prepare required legal filings. Time takes time, and even if your legal expert has done this same transaction hundreds of times, foreign governments change—their laws change, their administrative personnel change, their elected officials change—and each, and often all, of these changes will make your transaction different from the hundreds that preceded it.

Compliance Complications

Achaessa James, NCEO

Failure of compliance can be messy, expensive and embarrassing. Here are some examples of compliance failure: one a publicly embarrassing occurrence, one a potentially costly scenario, one a potential disaster, and one with unexpected consequences.

Embarrassing oversight. It was reported by *Forbes* in a September 19, 2009, news story[2] that in 2008 and 2009 the *New York Times* failed to take plan limits into consideration. The 1991 plan limits grants to 400,000 shares a year, but that didn't stop the Times from granting the CEO 650,000 shares in 2008 (and another 500,000 in 2009!) as well as 500,000 for the chairman. And, as if that wasn't enough, the Times also granted performance awards with a potential payout greater than the plan limit. Oops!

---

2. "New York Times Co. retracts exec stock options, issues correction after breaking own rules," *Forbes,* September 19, 2009, www.forbes.com.

Expensive oversight. Section 6039 requires information statements to be furnished in writing to employees and ex-employees who exercise an ISO or dispose of ESPP stock in addition to reporting the transaction to the IRS. This isn't just a helpful service to employees, this is a legal requirement, and a costly one for non-compliant companies. Penalties include:

- $50 for each failure to furnish a correct payee statement, up to a maximum of $100,000 per calendar year.
- In the case of intentional disregard of the reporting requirements, $100 per failure with no maximum.
- Failure to provide the IRS with copies of the statements is $50 per failure up to a maximum of $250,000 per year.

Disastrous oversight. IRC Section 422 requires that incentive stock options (ISOs) be granted only to active employees. Many boards authorize ISO grants to incoming employees *before* the scheduled hire date—making the grants non-compliant with IRC Section 422. A pattern of making non-compliant grants can disqualify the entire plan and all ISO grants made under it. If the plan is disqualified, all ISO-holding employees would lose the tax-qualified status of their grants!

Unexpected consequences. Technology is a great time saver, but all too often we rely on it to think like a human. A good example is the common lack of coordination between payroll programs and equity administration programs. The HR department notifies the payroll department to input an employee termination, but without internal controls in place the equity administration department never gets notified. Former employees who improperly show as active in the equity administration database continue to show options as vesting and accrual of associated compensation expense. Depending on the size of the company and the infrequency of reconciliations, such oversights can skew financials by hundreds of thousands of dollars. The 2010 passage of the Dodd-Frank Act now requires that, in the event of restatement due to material noncompliance of the company with any financial reporting requirement under the securities laws, the company will recover from any current or former officer who received incentive-based compensation (including stock options) during the three-year period preceding the restatement, based on erroneous data, any excess compensation (over and above what the executive would have received under the restated numbers.) Even if the restatement turns out to be non-material, or the equity compensation ends up increasing because of the restatement (instead of decreasing), restating prior financials or footnoting current financials can incur a large expense to investigate the issue and is likely to incite shareholder suspicion.

Lessons

In each of the above examples, the easy key to compliance is two-fold:

- *Appropriate staffing.* Equity compensation professionals must be trained to keep their stock plans in compliance, and that means having an intimate knowledge of the core disciplines of equity compensation: accounting; equity plan design, analysis and administration; corporate and securities law; and taxation.
- *Stakeholder communication.* Equity compensation administration requires the cooperation of key corporate departments—legal, HR, payroll, tax, and finance. A qualified equity compensation professional understands the importance of building strong internal controls that include consistent interaction among key players and regular periodic reporting that gets reviewed by a qualified individual.

Human Resourceful

Jennifer George, Orrick, Herrington & Sutcliffe LLP

As an outside legal professional, I often get asked for support when an in-house plan administrator can't get its human resource department to cooperate or when the HR department wants an outside "voice of authority."

Promises, promises. I frequently get calls from panicky stock plan professionals informing me that HR promised someone in x or y country stock options, ESPP participation, etc. HR's job sometimes seems to be more focused on getting talented people hired than worrying about small details like "is it legal?" to make the promised grants (and on the terms promised) to the new hires. Sometimes the company goes forward anyway, depending on the country and the risk level, and sometimes revisions have to be made to the planned grants to grant an alternative equity vehicle or cash award.

Too many cooks in the kitchen. I worked with one large U.S. multinational corporation that was rolling out a new benefit program globally, in 40 or so countries. The corporation decided that it would be a good idea to get "buy in" from the locals in each country before rolling out the plan, so it decided to set up calls with key locals in each country to explain the proposed terms of the program, etc. (I was less than supportive about this idea for rolling out the plan, but not everyone listens to their legal counsel!) I dutifully participated in each conference call with the locals to help explain how the plan would work and answer questions that the locals had about the proposed program. Not surprisingly, some of the locals had their own ideas about what the terms of the plan should be, how it should be communicated, and, in some countries, their ideas were quite creative. Although "tweaks" were made in some countries to accommodate local tax or legal issues, my contacts at U.S. headquarters had no intention of offering the plan differently in every country outside the U.S. just because the locals had a different idea of what they thought the terms should be. So, more conference calls were set up to discuss various "suggestions" that were received from the locals. I wasn't sure how these calls were going to go, but soon my wondering was over. They went something like this, "We understand that you thought that the plan should have x terms, and Jennifer will tell you why we can't do it that way." Ah, ha. A good use for outside counsel...

Lessons

Seasoned equity compensation professionals will be diligent in making friends with HR to find out what's coming down the pipeline in advance of communicating anything to employees or potential employees. Superior equity compensation professionals will also do the following:

- Create or oversee the creation of educational materials for an HR audience to ensure that equity compensation information is clear and concise and that HR understands enough to know when to ask questions beforehand.
- Create or oversee the creation of educational materials for a general employee audience to ensure that equity compensation information is easy to understand and that employees are confident that HR and the equity compensation team work together to administer this valuable employee benefit.
- Organize regular stakeholder meetings that include key members of HR, legal, payroll, operations, the executive team, and equity compensation to ensure that there are never any surprises and that everybody gets what is needed on time and in the appropriate format.[3]

Do the Hokey-Pokey and Turn Yourself Around

Bruce Brumberg, myStockOptions.com

Q. Please help me make sense of my W-2, as I am starting to collect all the information needed for my tax return. Last year I exercised stock options and immediately sold the shares in a cashless exercise on the same day. I also had restricted stock that vested, and I made two purchases under my company's employee stock purchase plan. I still hold the shares from the restricted stock vesting and the ESPP purchase. Where does the income from these appear on my W-2?

A. First, nothing appears on your W-2 in connection with your ESPP, though ESPP taxation gets more complex when you sell the shares. For restricted stock or standard restricted stock units (RSUs), the income (i.e., the value of the shares at vesting) and withholding amounts are included in, and totaled with, all the same boxes in which your regular compensation appears. Though it is not required to, your company

3. The Equity Co-sourcing Delegation Checklist that accompanies the NCEO's *Private Company Equity Administration Handbook* (scheduled for publication in 2011) is a great tool for understanding the annual and periodic needs of all stakeholder groups.

may break out the amount of the restricted stock income in Box 14 ("Other"). If you had a grant of performance shares, the W-2 would be the same.

For stock options, the reporting can depend on whether you have nonqualified stock options (NSOs) or incentive stock options (ISOs). With ISOs, the amount will be part of your compensation income in Box 1. If you have state and local taxes, the amount will also be included in the boxes for these. However, no withholding applies to ISOs (taxes are still owed with your return), and you have no Social Security or Medicare income, so nothing should be included for the ISO exercise and stock sale on your W-2 (some states, such as Pennsylvania, are an exception). For NSOs, all the income (i.e., the spread at exercise) and withholding appear in the same boxes with your regular compensation income and withholding. The IRS does require that Box 12 (using Code V) must show the spread income at exercise for NSOs. If you also had stock appreciation rights (SARs), the reporting is similar to NSOs without the reporting in Box 12.

Lessons

The point of including this story is to emphasize the extreme importance of thorough, consistent and ongoing employee education, including having expert resources available to answer the sometimes complicated questions that arise.

Such expert resources don't have to be in-house staff people or even paid outside professionals like lawyers or CPAs; they just need to be reliable subject matter experts who can provide answers that are understandable to the recipient. The NCEO, the NASPP, a CEP's professional network, and professional firms that specialize in equity compensation issues are a good place to start. Your plan administrator should have access to these resources and should be able to get reliable answers and transmit them to your employees.

Here are a few ideas on how to disseminate educational and informational materials to employees:

- Have an online FAQ where the plan administrator can receive and respond to employee questions.

- Have a dedicated Web site where staff can download informational materials, including internal process instructions (e.g., how to exercise your options, how to sign up for ESPP participation, what is an 83(b) election?) and expert white papers on particularly complicated issues.
- Have a formal new hire training session with the plan administrator.
- Have periodic informational luncheons. Software vendors and your professional service providers will often provide an informational speaker for free.
- Have an annual "benefits fair," and invite HR and the equity administration team to staff tables and answer questions about such benefits as 401(k) plans, option plans, health savings accounts, flexible spending accounts, etc. Again, sometimes service providers will send experts to staff these events for free.

Chapter 5

Technology

Wait. Don't start issuing awards just yet. How will you keep track of them? Please don't say on a spreadsheet! As I've mentioned several million times by now, equity compensation is one of the most regulated and legislated activities on the planet. For each award, your plan administrator must be able to track its compliance with securities laws, accounting regulations, corporate and individual tax laws, domestic and foreign payroll tax laws, data privacy laws, SEC regulations, insider trading, trading windows, blackout periods, valuation standards, and on and on. You don't expect the administrator to keep all that information in his head, do you? That would be cruel and unusual punishment. Arming your equity compensation administrator with only a spreadsheet is tantamount to precisely that.

Up until the late 1990s, it was common practice for non-public company stock option plans to be tracked by corporate attorneys on spreadsheets. Unfortunately, there are still some firms and some companies that continue to use spreadsheets. Let's be clear about this—no matter how sophisticated your spreadsheet may be, it will never be able to provide the level of financial analysis required by ASC 718, nor will it ever meet your IT department's data security requirements or an auditor's internal control requirements.

But not just any technology will do. No technology is perfect, but a thorough vetting combined with written processes will keep your plan compliant, if not completely bug-free.

Spreadsheets Were Not Made To Do High-Impact Accounting Work

Takis Makridis, EquityMethods

A spreadsheet is a wonderful tool because it's easy to use—we all know how to get spreadsheets to do some pretty amazing things. It's a common language. Unfortunately, spreadsheets can be a risky platform on which to base equity award accounting—at least when the materiality of the equity awards to the P&L is sizable. Fundamentally, a spreadsheet is not a relational database that allows different data elements to be linked, merged, and then decoupled. However, this is precisely what occurs when a spreadsheet is used for equity award accounting—especially to true-up full/partial forfeitures, roll-forward the balance sheet DTA balance, track the APIC Pool, expense performance awards, and handle modifications.

One case comes to mind of a large health care company. It had been recording expense and deferred taxes using a common spreadsheet program. The expense spreadsheets were generally accurate, but after a number of years, the auditors began questioning the deferred tax balances. As it turns out, the deferred tax asset was misstated by almost $50 million. This unpleasant situation stemmed from the expense recognition model not being linked dynamically to the tax model. As a result, exercises and cancellations were not being consistently applied within the tax model. Further, because the tax model was computing a current period impact, there was no way to prove the cumulative balance. Proving the cumulative deferred tax balance is important because the balance sheet itself is stated in terms of ending balances and not current period activity.

Lessons

Ultimately, it doesn't particularly matter the type of system used to perform equity compensation accounting as long as the system chosen:

- is predicated on relational database principles and integrated across expense, tax, EPS, and disclosure calculations.
- dynamically handles the various events that happen to awards (exercises, cancellations, modifications, etc.).

Easy as Pi

Paul Leisey, EquityMethods

A mid-cap retail company with a broad-based employee equity compensation plan was calculating employee equity award expensing manually in a spreadsheet. However, this became overwhelming very quickly since this company had quite a number of awards with different vesting schedules and the awards were at different points in their life. The company convinced its auditors to let it expense the awards on a pool basis over the weighted average remaining vesting life.

The company used this method for a few quarters before deciding that it should use software to generate reports that were more granular. When implementing the new software, it was quickly discovered how wrong the simplified expensing spreadsheet was. Many hours were spent devoted to reconciling the software solution to the spreadsheet solution, and, ultimately, the company came to the conclusion that the corners that were cut were rather significant.

Lessons

The moral of the story is to fully understand the trade-offs between the ideal reporting solution and a simplified spreadsheet, because the simple method often ends up costing more heartache in the long run, and the expense to remedy the situation can exceed what it would have cost to do it properly from the beginning.

The Angry Billionaire

Dan Walter, Performensation Consulting

Someone walked into my office and simply said, "Mr. Smith is on the phone. He wants to talk to someone in management and he is really mad." Mr. Smith (not his real name) was the namesake of a successful public company. He was not known for his people skills.

I took the phone, introduced myself, and asked how I could help. He told me that the people he had talked to were useless. They couldn't tell him how much his options were worth and he found it unacceptable. When I checked the system, I saw the same thing as everyone else. Where the value of options normally appeared was just a string of asterisks. I asked if I could look into it and get back to him within the hour. He demanded an answer while he was on the phone. Oh, well.

I pulled out a good old-fashioned 10-key and started adding everything up. For each grant I calculated the current potential gain and then added up the subtotals. When I looked at the grand total, I realized we had found a small flaw in our software system. Our options values only went up to $999,999,999.99. That's right, it was 1998 and our system had never considered the possibility that someone could have more than $1 *billion* in exercisable options. I calmly got back on the phone and told Mr. Smith that he had just a little bit more than $2.6 billion in exercisable stock options. I also explained that we would have the system updated as soon as possible, but that for the immediate time, he could call me directly if he needed this number again. Rather than be excited that he had the information he wanted and that his values were higher than anything I had personally seen before (or since), he simply hung up on me.

Lessons

There are three primary lessons that I see here; two are a bit clichéd:

- In this technology-dependent work, sometimes the technology fails. Don't be caught off guard when your technology doesn't respond the way you expect it to. Be flexible, be honest, and be on top of working it out with your technology vendor.
- First impressions count. Whether you're an in-house administrator or a service provider, you really only get one chance with some people. Once they're mad, you won't be able to give them what they want. So don't take it personally, just be prepared.
- No number is big enough if someone expected a bigger one.

Scandalous Software

Kim Kovacs, OptionEase

Equity compensation software clients used to be primarily larger, public companies with unlimited resources. But, with accounting regulations becoming more complicated every year, vendors have seen a corresponding increase in private and smaller public companies looking for a technology solution to manage their equity compensation programs. It used to be that every time I met with a new prospect I was surprised that it was still handling its equity compensation on a spreadsheet, or a 20-year-old custom software program. Not any more. Now I am only surprised by the amount of time it takes for a company to finally reach a pain point strong enough to force it to seek a technology solution.

Take Company MNOP, for example. Founded in 1995, MNOP is an established leader as a provider of a Web-based technology that integrates any type of technology, on-premise, cloud, or vendor-hosted, to provide users a seamless computing experience across all of a company's business platforms. The CFO wasn't a bit embarrassed when he stated that the company still used a software program written by an IT consultant in 1999 and delivered reports on a spreadsheet. The only reason the company was looking for a new solution, he said, was because it was taking the accounting department four hours to run a single report for the board meeting—well, that and it just looked bad for a SaaS vendor to be using old technology. Once we talked, however, and he realized that the IT-developed program wasn't tracking any of the laws and regulations that affect equity issuance and expensing, and that noncompliance could be costly to both his company and his award recipients, he was not only embarrassed; he was horrified. In the end we put his plan into a technology that met all the company's compliance needs and also reduced its reporting time down to minutes.

Lessons

This is a great example of how often an accounting executive may be unaware of all the implications of having an equity compensation plan. Payroll companies have done a good job of conveying to the business world the complicated nature of administering payroll, with its tax withholding and payment, and tracking of sick leave, vacation time, disability leave, etc. Benefits administrators have done a similar job of demonstrating the complicated nature of administering other employment benefits, if only by the mountains of paper they distribute several times a year. And because of the obviously difficult task of managing these highly regulated processes, company executives know that there will be costs associated with the administration of these benefits and don't question too deeply when confronted with the bill. It's just a part of doing business.

On the other hand, the mechanics and costs of administering equity compensation plans seem to remain shrouded in mystery, and when that veil is pierced, business owners and executives are often caught off guard.

Historically, equity compensation administration for early stage, non-public companies was a relatively simple affair, often done on a spreadsheet by paralegals assisting corporate counsel. Most of the regulations to be followed were mechanical and easily monitored by the board and the CEO—grant only the number of shares authorized in the reserve pool, ISO grants only to employees, ISOs must be exercised within three months of employee termination, and other similar rules.

Shortly after the turn of the century, two events converged that would make spreadsheets not only unacceptable, but potentially dangerous—the backdating scandal of 2006, and the mandatory application of ASC Topic 718 (formerly FAS 123(R)) to equity compensation in non-public companies beginning in fiscal years starting after December 15, 2005.

What were once simple awards now require data security, audit trails, and complicated accounting calculations. Even if only the essential requirements are met, being able to prove that awards were made on a certain date when the stock price was a specific amount requires tracking the issue date and the processing date (thus the need for data security and an audit trail). Calculating the fair value of an equity compensation award requires the use of an option-pricing model based on six factors, several of which require analysis of historic grant and forfeiture patterns, and, thus, tracking of employee termination dates and forfeitures, expiration and exercise dates, and the time elapsed between the grant date and the forfeiture, expiration, or exercise date. These factors emphasize the need for an auditable solution that calculates the expense based on all of these factors, appropriately weighted to the company's circumstances. Add to these basics the requirement of equity accounting for some awards (e.g. options granted to employees) and liability accounting for other awards (e.g. non-employee NSOs), and auditors requiring straight-line expensing for some awards and tranche-based expensing for others, plus compliance with valuation issues presented by Internal Revenue Code Section 409A, and the myriad opportunities for losing control of this complicated activity become evident.

The enactment of these regulations has produced a corresponding increase in the technology available for complying with them. Legacy software vendors created expense calculation programs to add to or sell with existing products. New vendors wrote comprehensive expensing programs into administration software that also cross-checks against other regulatory variables. While these technologies are more expensive than using a spreadsheet, the advent of cloud computing opened the door for them to be delivered over the Internet, thus eliminating the need for expensive software updates each time the regulations change.

Depending upon the number of plan participants and the specific functionality that meets your company's needs, technology fees can range from a few thousand dollars per year into the tens of thousands of dollars per year. When you are selecting a technology, it is most important to make sure that the program meets your company's specific needs. If your company is a public company, you'll need a program with a broker interface and a strong proxy reporting module. If your company is private, you'll need a program with robust cap table reporting for tracking all your stock, warrants, and equity compensation awards. Any program will need to have an expensing module that has been accepted by your audit firm.[1]

Then, of course, you'll need someone qualified to do the actual administration, monitor the database, and take ownership of the expensing process. It is highly important to select a qualified individual as your administrator—someone who understands all of the underlying issues and the interplay between tax, accounting, finance, securities laws, human resources, and plan design and administration issues. A direct hire of such a professional can be expensive and may not be economically feasible for early-stage companies.

Fortunately, there are several outsourcing alternatives, with a wide range of fees; just be sure that whoever is in charge of the administration has the Certified Equity Professional designation awarded by the CEP Institute at Santa Clara University (http://www.scu.edu/business/cepi/). The CEP is the only professional certification for the equity compensation industry. It ensures that your administrator has a clear

1. The NCEO's *Private Company Equity Administration Handbook* (scheduled for publication in 2011) will include a CD with useful documents such as a technology needs assessment and platform comparison.

understanding of all equity compensation issues and a network of expert-level resources in the industry.

In conclusion, administration of equity compensation awards demands the same high level of professionalism and exactitude as administration of any other employee benefit program, and the costs of administration need to be included when factoring the overall cost of the benefit plan. The expense of failing to put a priority on proper administration can be calculated in elevated audit fees and, worst case, penalties and interest assessed by the Internal Revenue Service or disqualification of your entire equity compensation plan.

Timing Is Everything

Robyn Shutak, NASPP
Achaessa James, NCEO

François de la Rochefoucauld said, "The only thing constant in life is change." Four hundred years later that maxim is even truer as technological advances make the programs we use obsolete the day after we implement them and, for equity compensation administrators, regulatory and legislative requirements change as soon as we get a real handle on them. The benefit—such constant change encourages your administrator to keep current with continuing education programs. The challenge—what to do when your software vendor upgrades the stock administration program? Here are two avoidable stories.

The first is an example of what can happen when the company uses an on-premise software:

Company GHI still has its ESPP. The company IT department maintains the program and the database on servers on the 13th floor of HQ. The software vendor makes a new release available on Monday and the stock plan department upgrades its system on Tuesday. Sample reports are run, and all the numbers reconcile.

On Thursday, the stock plan administrator processes an ESPP purchase in the upgraded system but isn't able to save her work. The dominoes start to fall—she can't save it, she can't transfer share allocation information to the captive broker, she can't distribute purchase details to participants or the internal department managers. By 6 p.m., the software vendor still hasn't been able to identify the issue. By the following Tuesday the software vendor finally has a "patch" that enables the administrator to save the purchase. The vendor's other clients receive a technical alert advising them of a bug in the software upgrade.

The second example is what can happen when the company uses Web-based software:

Company LMN also has an ESPP. Its Web-based program will be updated by the vendor that hosts the program on Tuesday. The stock administrator knows that he'll be processing an ESPP purchase on Thursday, so he has spoken in advance with the software vendor to ensure that there will be no change that affects his ESPP purchase activities. The vendor assures him that the new release is addressing other parts of the system and the ESPP functionality won't be affected. Thursday comes, and for some reason the FTP uploader won't accept the data upload. The stock administrator reviews the text file, checks all the formatting and coding, can't find anything wrong with the data, and reports the problem to the vendor using the online incident system. An hour later, he starts calling the vendor and is assured that its staff is working on it. He calls every two hours thereafter. By 4 p.m. the problem has still not been resolved, and the stock administrator decides to begin entering the purchases by hand—all 2,157 of them, one at a time. At 6:30 p.m., after two and a half hours of grueling data entry, the vendor emails the stock administrator to say that it found the problem and the FTP uploader is functional again. The stock administrator now has to decide whether he wants to spend his time manually deleting all of the transactions he just entered or manually checking them all in order to leave them in the system.

Lessons

There is no doubt that technology makes our lives easier, but there are still times when we rely on it more than we should or in ways that we shouldn't. In each of the above situations, the administrators did what they thought was necessary to ensure that the upgrade would go smoothly—in the first example, the stock administrator reconciled the numbers, and in the second example the administrator got assurances from the vendor well in advance—but both of them failed to take the most important step of actually testing the functionality in a test environment before the ESPP purchase.

Here are a couple of other important things to keep in mind when considering a software change or upgrade:

- If you can control the implementation date, schedule it so that you have enough time to thoroughly test the software before processing any time-sensitive transactions.
- The QA testers on the vendor's technology team don't use the software in the same way you do, and users often find bugs and programming errors that slip right by the most diligent quality check, so don't assume that because the vendor says the upgrade won't interfere with your transaction that your activity will be trouble free.
- And, it's worth repeating, make sure that you have a test environment separate and apart from your main database where you can try out the functionality of the new release first. Do the test in exactly the same way you would do the real transaction, and do it as far in advance as possible.

Chapter 6

Tax and Law

Now you can start issuing awards. But it's no time to relax. This is when compliance with tax regulations and securities laws is scrutinized. These are the kinds of stories that make you gasp, the real horror stories of equity administration. These are the stories that make the news.

The Plan Says What?!?

Mike Stevens, Alston & Bird LLP

An international company had a long-standing equity program, making annual grants of options and restricted stock units (RSUs) to employees in several countries. At one point in the past, a wealthy U.S.-based employee asked to receive awards in the form of restricted stock so that the employee could make an 83(b) election.

An 83(b) election allows the employee to pay taxes based on the stock price at the date of grant, rather than as the award vests. This is a risky proposition when the value of the stock is substantial because any forfeiture of the shares (due to termination of employment or other failure to vest), or any decrease in the share price, will mean that the employee overpaid his or her taxes. Even worse, the employee does not receive a tax refund on the overpaid amount. The upside is that, if the employee vests in the shares and the stock price increases, all of the gain is taxed at capital gains rates, rather than ordinary income. An 83(b) election is not available for restricted stock units—it is available only for restricted stock, and restricted stock is not eligible for grant in many foreign jurisdictions.

In a desire to accommodate the employee but discourage a host of U.S. employees from seeking restricted stock for non-financial reasons, the company amended the plan to provide that U.S. participants could receive restricted stock instead of RSUs, but only if they would file an 83(b) election with respect to the award.

Several years later, the company hired a new CEO. The company offered a sizeable equity award upon hire, and the CEO requested restricted stock so that he could hold outstanding shares.

After a few weeks, the company called its compensation lawyer:

"Just wanted to let you know that we brought the new CEO in. He started two weeks ago. I can send you a copy of his agreement for your files. We just worked the agreement through our labor lawyers–it's pretty much in line with our standard agreements."

"So what did he get as an initial grant?"

"Half a million in restricted stock."

"He filed an 83(b) election on half a million dollars' worth of restricted stock? Your current value is over $10 per share. That's crazy."

"Um, what are you talking about?"

The CEO wasn't about to file an 83(b) election. The in-house staff who had written the odd provision into the plan had forgotten that it was there. The lawyers working the agreement (on both sides) hadn't read the plan. After all, the plan authorized the issuance of restricted stock—who would have guessed that the requirements for the grant went deeper than that?

Unfortunately, the grant was technically outside of the plan requirements. To avoid any issues about the validity of the award, the compensation committee was reconvened, the plan was amended, and the grant was re-issued. The episode was an unfortunate embarrassment to many of the people involved.

Lessons

When issuing an award, keep in mind all of the various policies and plan requirements that may come into play. If you have adopted a grant policy, you may not be able to grant the award right now. If your plan requires a three-year vesting requirement for awards, you might not be able to cut a deal with a new employee. If you have an employee-only plan, then you will have to find some other way to make a grant to a consultant. And if your crazy plan says that you can only issue restricted stock if the participant files an 83(b) election, then you've got some issues to discuss before you make a large grant to your new CEO.

These things seem silly, but they happen. They happen to smart, well-intentioned people who just get used to granting the same thing over and over. It's easy to expect the same requirements to apply in every circumstance, especially when the hidden provision is unusual, hasn't been invoked in years, and was drafted by a person in-house who has long since moved on.

A well-drafted plan will give the board or the compensation committee broad authority to set the terms of an award. But issuing an award that directly flies in the face of a plan requirement is trouble. Sometimes people will argue that if the board authorized the new award, then that's tantamount to a one-off amendment for this particular award. But most of the time when this sort of thing occurs, the board was not aware that it was stepping outside of the plan requirements. As the requirements were placed there for a reason, it behooves the board to consider the circumstances and to determine whether an exception to the requirement is appropriate and how it should be implemented.

To 83(b) or Not to (b)...What Was the Question?

Fred Whittlesey, Hay Group

Stock compensation does not become taxable until there is no longer a risk that the recipient may lose the stock—it's called a "substantial risk of forfeiture." Since stock grants that have vesting requirements can be forfeit anytime until the vesting requirement is met, under Section 83 of the Internal Revenue Code, they aren't taxable at the time of grant. When the stock vests, then the difference between what the recipient paid for the stock (sometimes nothing) and the fair market value on the date of vesting becomes taxable ordinary income. If the price of the stock goes up a lot, then the grant recipient could potentially have a large amount of income and an associated large tax bill.

The IRS also provides a way to accelerate the recognition of the taxable compensation by allowing the grant recipient to file what's known as a Section 83(b) election within 30 days of the date of grant. The 83(b) election basically says that even though the stock isn't vested, the grant recipient is willing to claim the income at the time of filing the election and pay the taxes now as if the stock were vested.

Filing an 83(b) election is basically a bet by the taxpayer that the stock price is going to rise dramatically. Filing the election is very commonly done by founders and executives in startup companies who receive the stock when the value is extremely low. As the following story illustrates, filing an 83(b) election when the stock price is not extremely low can have expensive consequences.

When Company B was first formed as a spinoff from its parent company, large restricted stock grants were issued to all of the executives. The executives all filed 83(b) elections for the grants, reasoning that it was better to pay ordinary income taxes on the value of the stock now than it would be to pay taxes on both the value of the stock and the appreciation of the stock at the time of vesting three years later. Plus filing the 83(b) election at grant would mean that any gain on the later sale of the stock would be taxed at the lower capital gains rate.

The stock was trading at around $80 per share at the time of grant, and the high-salaried executives averaged $32 per share in taxes. At some point during the vesting period, the market imploded and the stock dropped to around $20 a share. In the end the executives had paid $32 per share in taxes to receive $20 per share in value. Because there is no refund of overpaid 83(b) election taxes, the executives had only the tax benefit of a long-term capital loss to compensate them. And depending upon how much total loss was incurred, that loss might have to be spread out over several years to recoup entirely. In this case, the stock basis was $80 per share, the sale price was $20 per share, resulting in a capital loss of $60 per share. The capital loss limit for any one year is only $3,000, so one of these executives selling as few as 51 shares would have more capital loss than could be claimed in one year.

The only other remedy would be to hold on to the stock and hope that the value would rise again.

Lessons

The notion of possible tax savings is attractive but must be carefully explored under all scenarios to ensure that the risk being assumed is reasonable.

Let's recap the conditions for using an 83(b) election:

- The election must be filed within 30 days of the grant.
- Taxes are due on the difference between the amount paid for the stock and the fair market value on the day of the election (if any), which is taxed as ordinary income.
- The taxpayer must pay the taxes with the filing of the election.
- If the stock is forfeit before vesting, then there is no refund of taxes paid on the forfeit shares.
- If the value of the stock is lower at the time of vesting than on the date of grant, there is no refund of the taxes paid at the time of filing the election.
- If the value of the stock has increased between the time of filing the election and the sale of the stock, the gain is treated as capital gain.
- If the value of the stock has decreased between the time of filing the election and the sale of the stock, the loss is treated as capital loss.

So was the risk assumed in this example "reasonable"? From that perspective, it only makes sense to pay taxes if (a) the taxable amount at grant is low, and (b) the reasonably expected increase in stock price between the grant date and the vesting date is high. Was $80 per share "low"? What would be a reasonable increase in share price that could justify paying taxes in advance?

Sometimes It's All Bad News...

Steve Kifer, CEP, Jefferies & Company

A few years ago, when the economic crisis of 2008 was just beginning to cause the collapse of some major companies, I did some consulting work for a company in a highly affected sector. The recurring annual restricted stock grants to the directors had been made at the beginning of the year, and each of the directors filed an 83(b) election. Midway into the year, the crisis started to seriously affect the company, and one of the directors resigned as a result of disagreements on how to handle the problems. The resignation resulted in a forfeiture of all of his unvested restricted stock. Somehow, this director didn't realize that when he filed the 83(b) election on the restricted stock he had to pay income taxes on the $500,000 value of the unvested stock grant.

Early in the next calendar year, as we were prepping the 1099s, I had to make the unfortunate call to him to let him know that we would be reporting the $500,000 income. It wasn't until then that he realized that he would have to pay approximately $100,000 in taxes and, even worse, he still had to pay it even though he would now never receive the stock.

Lessons

In this case, I think it was a combination of the lack of communication to the director about the effects of filing an 83(b) and his lack of understanding about the 83(b) in general that eventually cost him over $100,000 in taxes that he had to pay. As a result of this, I worked with our corporate counsel to prepare an informational memo on 83(b) elections that included a summary of the tax law, some examples of what could happen when an 83(b) election is filed and, of course, a disclaimer that the memo should not be taken as tax advice but that the recipient should consult his or her own tax professional for the effect of filing an 83(b) election on his or her personal tax situation.

Timing Is Everything No. 2

Achaessa James, NCEO

It's one thing to fail to turn in something to your payroll department on its timeline. It's another thing to forget to pay the IRS on its timeline.

In September 2008, Joe Camello, CEO at GH Inc., received a restricted stock unit grant that would vest in full 12 months from the grant date. GH Inc. had a very good year in 2008. So good that CEO Camello's annual bonus was $900,000. Joe received his bonus in January 2009, just in time to buy tickets to Super Bowl XLIII. Joe was a big Arizona Cardinals fan. Alas, the game was a bust.

On September 1, the stock administrator was reviewing the upcoming month's award vesting report and noticed that Joe's RSU payout of $500,000 was scheduled for the next day. She checked the equity administration database and confirmed that Joe's annual salary was $400,000, and his average annual bonus was $300,000, so the RSU payout wouldn't put him over the $1 million limit for supplemental income tax withholding payment, then notified payroll about the payout and reminded payroll that taxes should be withheld at the supplemental tax rate of 35%.

The junior payroll clerk called Joe. He explained that they could either order a hand cut check for the $325,000 after-tax payout or run the payout through the September 15 payroll along with the withholding. Joe, feeling better than he'd felt since the Cardinals' loss in February, asked for a hand-cut check instead of waiting.

The payroll clerk reported the RSU payout to the payroll service in the next regular payroll run on September 10. Imagine the payroll department supervisor's expression when the payroll service provider called about the deposit of the $175,000 supplemental income withholding taxes for Joe's payout. Because of his unusually large January bonus, Joe's RSU payout had pushed him over the $1 million supplemental income limit, and the taxes on the RSU payout should have been deposited with the IRS the day after the payout date. She asked if they wanted to deposit the already overdue $175,000 supplemental income withholding taxes immediately or wait until the regular payroll deposit on September 15. The service provider recommended waiting until September 15 because the payment had already missed the first penalty tier (2% for one to five days late) and five more days wouldn't make it any worse, but the 5% penalty ($8,750) should be deposited at the same time.

Lessons

Much like the CEO, the IRS wants its money at the first opportunity. We have three failures in this example:

- *Failure to coordinate.* Once again, we have a plan administrator who has failed to plan ahead to take the payroll schedule into consideration. Remember, even though you provide financial reports at month end, it is a good idea to review cash-based award payouts in coordination with the payroll schedule. In this example, the September 2 payout would still have been made between payroll submission dates, but if the payout date had been on September 1 the administrator could have planned ahead to have it pay out and have the withholding deposited on the regular September 1 pay date.

- *Failure of communication.* Some equity administration programs now have interfaces to integrate with payroll systems, but it has not yet become industry-wide practice. When these systems are not integrated, it is important to get regular downloads from the payroll system if the equity administration database will be involved in calculating the taxes on equity compensation transactions, especially if there is a chance that any executives will have substantial bonus income. As in this example, even if the equity administration database was not used for calculating withholding taxes, if the administrator had received payroll downloads she would have noticed the supplemental income and been able to alert the payroll clerk instead of relying on a simple note in the system about average bonus amounts to this participant.
- *Failure of knowledge.* When dealing with equity compensation, some of which is reportable as supplemental income, the stakeholders in all departments must have enough experience to at least know what questions to ask. In this example, the junior payroll clerk did not have a clear understanding of payroll withholding in the context of supplemental income. The equity administrator assumed that the payroll clerk would know to check the exact amount of the participant's supplemental income, and the clerk did not know enough about supplemental income to do so.

In Recognition of Your Dedicated Service, Please Accept this Excise Tax

Mike Stevens, Alston & Bird LLP

A private company issued restricted stock units under its incentive plan. The units had a three-year cliff vest based upon continuing employment and required that shares be distributed within 60 days following vesting. Accordingly, the awards met the requirements for the "short-term deferral" exemption under Section 409A of the tax code because the distribution would always be made prior to March 15 of the year following the year in which the awards vested.

One year after the grants were made, a longtime employee put in his retirement notice. The compensation committee decided that it would accelerate the employee's awards and make the distribution of shares immediately, in consideration of the employee's years of service. Because the award was exempt as a short-term deferral, acceleration of vesting *and immediate payout* did not raise any issues under 409A.

The committee then decided to add a retirement provision to the incentive plan to apply to future retirement scenarios, but with a slight (but important) difference. This retirement provision indicated that upon retirement, an employee's vesting would accelerate (so that the employee would not forfeit the award), *but the distribution schedule would remain the same.*

Several years later, another employee retired and asked that she be able to receive the shares immediately. The compensation committee agreed and took special action to authorize the immediate distribution following the accelerated vesting.

Lessons

Retirement acceleration provisions can be particularly problematic for time-based restricted stock units under 409A. Once an employee is retirement eligible, he or she is considered to be "vested" for purposes of determining deferrals under 409A. In a nutshell, retirement in this case would constitute voluntary termination, and any amount receivable upon voluntary termination is not considered to have a substantial risk of forfeiture under 409A. That is not to say that the employee is contractually vested under the award agreement—it just means that you have to consider the award to have vested when determining whether it constitutes deferred compensation under 409A.

In this case, the company's retirement provision required termination after age 55 and 10 years of service. The second retiree had met those requirements when the award was issued to her. Under a 409A analysis, her award was not an exempt short-term deferral because the award was considered to be "vested" for 409A purposes upon grant and the normal payout schedule contemplated payment after the third year.

While the retiree's award, as drafted, was compliant with 409A (the fixed payout schedule was permitted under 409A), 409A does not allow any discretionary acceleration of the distribution of any amounts of deferred compensation. Accordingly, acceleration of her payout would cause a 409A violation. Among other things, this would add a 20% excise tax penalty on top of her normal tax bill for the restricted stock unit. Always be mindful of retirement accelerators, and make sure that you consider their impact under 409A.

On the Road with Options

Bruce Brumberg, myStockOptions.com

As the "workplace" becomes more flexible to include remote employees and employees who have lengthy assignments in out-of-state satellite offices, it's important to remember that income from some option exercises is taxable and that each state has its own tax laws.

Q. I may leave my company to become a consultant and move to another state. Will there still be withholding on my nonqualified stock options (NSOs) as when I was an employee? Does it matter that I will live in another state when I exercise them?

A. As a general rule, most companies base withholding on your employment status at the time of grant. In other words, because you were an employee at the time of grant, federal and state taxes, along with Social Security and Medicare, will be withheld when you exercise.

If you were always an independent contractor, taxes will not be withheld at the time of exercise. You will receive a year-end 1099 to use for your personal tax filing. However, if you become an employee before you exercise your options, taxes will be withheld at exercise.

As for state taxation: each state determines the issue individually. Often, a state will tax options that are exercised by a person who was employed in that state when he or she received the options, even if he or she is not a resident at the time of exercise or sale of stock. New York, for example, taxes nonresidents on option exercises to the extent that the income on exercise is attributable to New York services.

Lessons

Let's take this example a bit further for the sake of demonstrating how domestic and global mobility can make employee withholding resemble a jigsaw puzzle. There are states and countries in which the income on an option exercise is taxable in proportion to the amount of time the person lived in the state/country while the option was vesting, whether or not he or she lived in the state/country at the time of grant or exercise. Did you follow that? Here's a more visual example:

Employee A lives in the U.S. in state G when an option is granted and for the first year of a four-year vesting schedule. In years two and three, Employee A lives in state M. In year four, Employee A is transferred to a foreign subsidiary in country X. In year five, Employee A comes back to the U.S. and resides in state W, where he exercises the option. Here are the tax laws that must be investigated by the payroll department to ascertain which taxation authority receives taxes on which percentage of the gain from the option exercise:

- U.S., state G: at option grant and for 12 months of service during vesting.
- U.S., state M: 24 months of service during vesting.
- Country X: 12 months of service during vesting.
- U.S., state W: 0 months of service during vesting, state of residence upon exercise.

The payroll department will have to consult tax experts in each U.S. state and country X to determine if the taxing authorities require:

- Taxation of the full amount of income upon exercise regardless of where the employee resided when the option was granted.
- Taxation of the full amount of income upon exercise regardless of where the employee resided when the option was exercised.
- Taxation of the income in proportion to the amount of time the employee resided or worked in the state/country while the option was vesting.

Trickled All The Way Down

Bruce Brumberg, myStockOptions.com

Q. I have about 12,000 stock options in a company that may have backdated more stock options than just those of the senior executives. How does this backdating affect me and the taxation of my stock grants?

A. At a minimum, do not expect any new stock option grants with a market price lower than the price on the grant date unless these are explicitly allowed by your stock plan and have been approved by the board of directors. Some of the companies involved in backdating have restricted employees from exercising outstanding stock options or buying stock through ESPPs, as examined by an article in the *San Francisco Chronicle.*[1]

The S-8 registration statement the company filed with the SEC for the shares issued under the stock plan is no longer current because the financial statements it references need to be restated for the backdating. Most stock plans have a provision that allows a company to stop issuing stock or options if it cannot do so, and some companies interpret the invalidation of the S-8 registration statement as grounds for triggering this provision. For any shares you own, the problem will escalate if trading in your company's stock is suspended, the shares are de-listed, and the stock price drops.

The tax issues depend on the type of grant you received, on whether you have exercised options already, and on future IRS guidance. One of the requirements for incentive stock options (ISOs) is that they cannot be granted at a discounted price. Therefore, any ISOs among your grants may have been disqualified. If you have held the shares long enough after exercise to receive the special ISO tax treatment, any capital gains tax you paid for the ISO stock sale may be converted in part back to ordinary income. Plus, taxes should have been paid at exercise, as these are now really nonqualified stock options (NSO), including withholding for Social Security and Medicare.

For backdated options granted as NSOs, your spread at exercise was larger than it otherwise might have been because you had a lower

1. "Hidden Victims of Option Backdating," *San Francisco Chronicle,* October 26, 2006, http://www.sfgate.com/cgi-bin/article.cgi?f=/c/a/2006/10/26/BUGHQLVSEI1.DTL.

exercise price than the market price on the grant date. With this bigger spread, you paid more taxes at ordinary income rates, but then again your gains were larger. Options that vest on or after January 1, 2005, face additional problems under Section 409A of the American Jobs Creation Act, as discounted options are taxed at vesting (with a potential tax penalty of 20% and interest), not at exercise. Backdated options exercised in 2006 trigger these penalties.

After an SEC investigation into backdating at Brocade Communications Systems, the company made a tender offer to its employees (see the Schedule T-0, filed with SEC) that let them exchange backdated options either for cash equal to the Black-Scholes value or for options repriced to the fair market value on the grant date plus cash equal to the eliminated discount. Other companies with unvested backdated options are expected to take a similar approach.

Lessons

Even though the backdating scandal has generally resolved itself, this story is included as a warning of how errors that lead to a restatement of financial reports will invalidate the company's S-8 registration statement which, in turn, affects the ability of all option recipients to exercise their vested awards and sell the shares obtained in the exercise. It is clear from the way corporate activities have been covered over in the recent past that some executives think business ethics violations can be hidden or minimized. With the passing of the Dodd-Frank Act in 2010, which requires the disgorgement of certain compensation elements by executive management in the event of financial restatements, a little bit of transparency has been added. The above example is meant to provide a clear reminder that even if the janitor or the receptionist don't see their names in newsprint, a corporate scandal can affect every employee in a company, whether or not the actor intended it.

Timing Is Everything No. 3

Achaessa James, NCEO

As a result of Martha Stewart's conviction, most people have heard of the insider trading portion of Section 16 Securities Exchange Act of

1934—using material non-public information to inform stock trading decisions—and know that violation of the insider trading regulations can result in criminal charges. But Section 16 has several more equally important requirements and prohibitions, and the corporate officers, directors, and certain executives and other employees who qualify as Section 16 reporting persons or insiders can have a challenging time staying in compliance. Section 16(b), for example, was enacted to prevent company insiders from making a profit on short-term trading in the stock of their own companies. Imagine the following:

A company's board decides that certain high-level corporate executives and officers have to own a minimum number of shares to ensure that they have "skin in the game." One of the corporate executives is short on holdings, so she executes a purchase of 50,000 shares of stock on the open market on April 1 at $13 per share to satisfy the company's new ownership requirements. On August 30, she decides to buy a new car and executes a same-day sale exercise, selling 10,000 shares of her exercised stock options at $19 per share. Because the August sale is only four-plus months from the April purchase, this is a "matchable" transaction, and $60,000 in profits must be disgorged.

In the real world, these numbers can quickly escalate. InfoSpace founder Naveen Jain is the proud owner of one of the largest settlement rulings. The judgment was for $247 million, although he settled for $105 million.[2] (Yes...that's million!) In a shareholder lawsuit filed in 2003, a lower court federal judge ruled that Jain had purchased shares of Infospace in violation of six-month short-swing insider trading rules and issued a $247 million judgment against him, the largest award of its kind at that time. While on appeal in 2005, Jain settled the case for $105 million while denying liability. Jain's attempt in further litigation to blame his former lawyers for the loss was dismissed. The Supreme Court refused to hear an appeal of the dismissal.

2. See "Settlement Agreement Reached in Infospace Derivative Case, Section 16(B) Case, and Certain Related Cases Brought by the Jains," http://www.sec.gov/Archives/edgar/data/1068875/000119312504219392/dex991.htm, and "Naveen Jain," *Wikipedia*, http://en.wikipedia.org/wiki/Naveen_Jain.

Lessons

Section 16(b) of the 1934 Act is one of the more complicated regulations. To avoid short-swing exposure, best practice calls for institution of a pre-clearance policy for all Section 16 reporting persons and persons with inside information, education for all persons covered by Section 16(b), and, need I add, a person knowledgeable about Section 16(b) to administer and enforce the company's stock programs. Here are the substantive components of Section 16(b):[3]

- Issuer stock is either sold and purchased, or purchased and sold, within any period of less than six months and does not qualify for one of the limited exemptions available.
- It is not a requirement that the insider realize actual profit on the transactions. Indeed, the calculation of profit on the sales and purchases is not based on sequential transactions, but instead is based on a matching of the highest price sale transaction to the lowest price buy transaction within any series of transactions that occur within any six month period. If multiple transactions occur within the six-month period, then all of the transactions are matched high sale to low buy.
- If a terminated or demoted individual was a reporting person, compliance with Section 16(b) will continue up to six months after the last transaction made while the individual was still a reporting person.
- Directors and officers are considered beneficial owners of issuer stock held by certain of their family members. Transactions by those family members can trigger a short-swing violation, and those transactions can be matched against the transactions of the director/officer or other covered family members.
- The public company cannot waive its right to recover short-swing profits. If a shareholder makes a demand that the company act to recover short-swing profits, the company has 60 days to do so or

3. Eric Orsic, "Federal Securities Law Considerations for Equity Compensation Plans," chap. 2 in *Selected Issues in Equity Compensation,* 8th ed. (Oakland, CA: NCEO, 2011), sec. 2.3.

the shareholder may bring suit to enforce the recovery on behalf of the company.

You Said, They Said, We Said...The Ambiguity Gremlin

Corey Rosen, National Center for Employee Ownership

One of the most common sources of litigation over equity awards is ambiguity about when and how to exercise. The ambiguity may arise from unclear plan or grant agreement language, from disagreement between the plan and the grant language, or from conflicts between what the grant agreement says and what someone in the company verbally or in writing told an employee could be done.

In *Gelhaus v. Fingerhut, Inc.* (Minn. Ct. Appl. May 7, 2002, unpublished), for instance, the plaintiff was the president of a subsidiary of Fingerhut. His employment agreement stated that he was entitled to "participate in" benefit plans for executives, including stock options. Fingerhut had advised Gelhaus that he was an employee of the subsidiary, not the parent, but he maintained that he had an ongoing employment agreement with Fingerhut. In 1999, Fingerhut was acquired by Federated Department Stores. Gelhaus tried to exercise his options but was denied. He sued, arguing that the employment agreement required that he be in the stock plan. The trial court and an appeals court agreed with Fingerhut that the employment agreement was ambiguous—too ambiguous, in fact, to construe without reference to plan documents. The documents gave discretion to a plan committee to decide who could get options. So score one for the company.

In *First Marblehead Corp. v. House,* No. 401 F. Supp. 2nd 152 (D. Mass. 2005), the plaintiff received a general memorandum from the company's legal counsel that described the terms of the plan (including a 10-year exercise period) but that did not explain what happened post-termination. Formal plan and grant documents were adopted later stating that the option had to be exercised within 90 days of termination. Six years after termination, House tried to exercise the options. The company said he could not. The court ruled for the company. Score two for the company.

But companies do not always prevail. In *Healy v. MCI WorldCom Network Services Inc.*, No. S-02-1575 LKK/DAD (E.D. Cal. Jan. 6, 2006), an executive claimed that his employment agreement superseded the grant agreement. The court ruled that the grant agreement was ambiguous about vesting, but the employment agreement was specific. The case hinged on Healy's statement about when he would have exercised the awards, and the court relied on that, awarding him interest and the gains he would have received.

In *Derek Lewitton v. ITA Software, Inc.*, No. 08-3725 (7th Cir. Oct. 28, 2009), a court ruled for the employee over whether his employment contract allowed him to exercise options. His agreement stated that some of his options would be forfeited if certain revenue goals for a project he was heading were not met. They weren't, but Lewitton claimed that it was because the project had been put on the back burner by the company. The contract specified that the vesting rule would be waived if the schedule for the project was "materially deferred." ITA contended that the term "materially deferred" was ambiguous and not meant to apply if the project was postponed in the way that it was. The court sided with Lewitton.

Lessons

Looking back over cases involving the ambiguity of various equity award documents, we found that employers almost always win. But winning can still be a loss because of legal costs, diversion of management time, and, if other employees know about the lawsuit, employee skepticism. The lesson, of course, is simple: make sure the terms are clear and consistent across all documents. That sounds easy, but with documents sometimes issued or amended at different times, with more than one person sometimes providing written material, and with the difficulty of defining certain terms (such as "materially"—a favorite lawyer word), it is not easy at all.

We Said One Thing, but We Wrote Another

Corey Rosen, National Center for Employee Ownership

Generally, courts have held that if what is clearly written in equity award agreements conflicts with what people were told by company officials (or claim to have been told), the written agreements, especially if they are signed, prevail. But as Corning, Lucent Technologies, Rencor Control, and other companies have learned in litigation (*Moses v. Corning Inc.,* No. 03-3003 [3rd Cir. July 16, 2004]; *Levy v. Lucent Technologies Inc.,* 2003 U.S. Dist. LEXIS 414, [S.D.N.Y. Jan. 14, 2003]; and *Cf. Ingram v. Rencor Control, Inc.,* No. 02-58-P-C [D. Me. Apr. 11, 2003]), this is not always the case, especially if there is any ambiguity at all in the documents and/or the parties making the oral representations agree they made them.

Lessons

People making oral representations need to be very, very sure they understand the agreements in their current form. Confusion often arises when the agreements have been amended. It is also wise always to tell the employee that in case of any conflicts, the written language prevails. Employees are well advised to get their own legal counsel to review any documents to make sure they are agreeing to what they think they are agreeing to.

It's Not the Activity but the Cover-Up That Gets You in Trouble

Achaessa James, NCEO

I could start this story with 50 case citations. Really. That's how many civil cases were brought by the Securities and Exchange Commission to prosecute companies and their executives for option backdating.

The end of 2010 saw the former CEO of KB Home sentenced to five years of probation in late November for his participation in covering up the improper accounting of backdated stock options, and the forfeiture of $47 million and payment of a $6 million fine to the SEC by the former CEO of Comverse, who had fled to Namibia in 2006 to avoid prosecution. These two cases brought to a close the once-hot topic of option backdating.

As reported in the *New York Times,* the backdating scandals brought to light in 2005 by a University of Iowa finance professor's research paper appeared at first to be easy pickings for the SEC and the Department of Justice (DOJ). More than 100 companies were investigated, approximately 150 companies issued financial restatements, dozens of company executives were terminated, and the SEC filed about 50 civil cases. Of the numerous criminal charges brought by the DOJ, however, the cases were simply too complex for prosecutors to effectively persuade juries and courts of the seriousness of the financial crimes. Indeed, the backdating itself was not illegal, but the improper accounting and tax treatment, and the cover ups to hide those activities, were. In the end, 12 executives were convicted of criminal activity, five received prison terms, and the remainder received probationary terms, with more than one court finding that the prosecution had failed to prove that the backdating had damaged the companies and their shareholders. A 2009 follow up to the initial research concluded that more than 2,000 companies that made executive stock option grants during the period 1996 through 2005 had manipulated the issuance of those awards.

Lessons

The principal lesson here is that the underlying activity—option backdating—is not illegal, per se. It is just not favorably looked upon by shareholders. In these cases, it was the decision by management to not be transparent about the backdating to shareholders, and the actions taken as a result of that decision, that caused the problem.

Thinking back for a moment to Graphic Packaging and the discussion about the costs of litigation, let us enumerate a few apparent, and sad, facts:

- The government has unlimited resources with which to prosecute alleged offenses.
- The defendants and their companies have limited resources.
- The courts generally agreed that the prosecutors had failed to prove that the backdating had damaged the companies and their shareholders.
- The litigation against the accused executives did have damaging consequences, such as executive terminations, tarnished professional reputations, tarnished corporate reputations, costly legal

fees paid by the companies, which reduced shareholder value, and angry and suspicious shareholders.

In summary, the truth may often be uncomfortable, but the scandal caused by a discovered untruthfulness is both costly and damaging.

Chapter 7

Accounting and Valuation

Accounting and valuation issues are less dramatic than the tax and law problems, but they provide the evidence that underlies the headlines. You don't want to slip up here, or it will cost you a bundle!

Don't Forget Sis

Mike Stevens, Alston & Bird LLP

It's the classic American success story. Two friends have a dream to build a new and innovative product. One of them has great vision, and the other has superior drive and management skills. They are well-intentioned and thoughtful in their approach. After securing some initial financing from friends and family, they quit their jobs, rent out some cool space in the back row of an office park, and the company is born.

On day one, there are seven shareholders—the two founders and five investors (each of their fathers, plus three family friends). They decide to keep things simple and issue only common stock. Though the company is worth very little up front, the investors come in at $1 per share, which is considered to be a "nice, round number."

On day two, one of the founders' sisters is brought on board as the first new employee. She has a marketing background, is savvy with the technology, and will play an important role in the fledgling company. The two founders meet with her and tell her that she will get "some sort of equity, once we figure out what to grant—probably options."

With the aid of some additional money from the investors (again, at $1 per share), the company grows. Engineers and tech staff are hired, a prototype is developed, and the new sales director starts making the rounds at industry events and product fairs. Reviews are good, and interest is high. The founders polish up their business plan and sales pitch, ready to hit the road to talk to big-money investors to get them through product launch. They also decide that the time has come to put an incentive plan in place for their dedicated employees.

After discussing various alternatives, the founders decide to issue stock options. Although the company's value is now believed to be around $.50 per share, they decide to issue options to employees at $1, so that they don't undercut the initial friends and family investors. Aside from the potential pricing pressure resulting from their soon-to-be sale of shares to outside investors, they have a more immediate problem: they forgot to issue the options to the sister.

Given the fact that the sister joined the company on day two, the founders would like to issue her options with an exercise price of $.01 per share. They know that the existing investors won't mind that, and the other employees will understand the pricing difference. At the time of grant, however, a penny option would be a discounted grant. The IRS takes the position that a deeply discounted stock option should be taxed as the grant of shares (i.e., when vested, rather than when the option is exercised). And besides that, any discounted grants are subject to Section 409A of the tax code, which severely limits the flexibility of stock options.

To pretend that the options were in fact issued back on day two would constitute "backdating" and would be completely contrary to the company's corporate records, its financial statements, and the offering memo that was used to raise money from friends and family. Because the founders failed to act timely and grant the awards when the company was new, their ability to fulfill the promise to the sister was severely limited.

Lessons

When it comes to stock options, pricing is important. Not only does it establish the floor that will determine the appreciation value of the option, but it plays a critical role in the accounting and legal treatment of the award.

There is no real guidance as to what constitutes a "deeply discounted" stock option. Most lawyers will tell you that a discount of 50% is troublesome, and going beyond that is downright problematic. But even a lesser discount will raise issues under Section 409A.

Section 409A of the Internal Revenue Code governs deferred compensation arrangements and limits the opportunity to make distribution of deferred amounts. Most stock options issued to a company's employees will be exempt from 409A, provided that the options are priced at or above the fair market value on the date of grant. Private companies must meet certain valuation requirements in determining the fair market value of their stock for grant purposes. It is very important that companies review these requirements and understand the impact of their pricing decisions. As a result of these rules, it is relatively rare to see discounted stock options any more.

If a discounted option is issued in violation of 409A, then, among other things, the employee will be subject to a special 20% excise tax, over and above the normal income tax that is due upon exercise (assuming that the option is not "deeply discounted").

In order to make a discounted option compliant with 409A to avoid this tax penalty (again, assuming that the option is not "deeply discounted"), the option may only be exercisable in certain pre-specified events that are included, up front, in a written grant agreement or the plan document. These events may include a time certain, the employee's separation from service, a change in control of the company, the participant's death or disability, or any combination of the foregoing.

For example, an option agreement could specify that the option is exercisable in a given year or, if earlier, upon the employee's separation from service. But neither the company nor the employee could determine that the option was exercisable at any other time. For example, if the original schedule did not indicate that the option could be exercised in the event of a change in control, then the company cannot accelerate exercise in the event a change in control occurs. In short, the exercise schedule would have to be set in stone at the time of grant.

This sort of pre-determined schedule can work in many instances, but it does not lend the kind of flexibility in exercise that is inherent in normal option awards.

Don't let a delay in timing impact the financial benefit you intend to deliver to your employees or to introduce legal complexities that complicate the terms of your award. When you decide to issue equity awards, you should always try to grant them as soon as possible, especially if you expect the stock price to increase in the near future.

It Was So Much Easier Just to Use a Formula for Valuation

Corey Rosen, National Center for Employee Ownership

Electrifying Concepts (not a real company, but one based on many very real ones I have spoken with) was a young entrepreneurial company that shared equity with most of its employees. The company was not traded on a stock market, and it did not have venture capital investment. Its CFO, Esther Novella, persuaded the board and the CEO that the best way to determine the price of the shares was either net asset value or a formula Esther had heard at the recent electronics parts wholesalers' trade show of two times sales. The board was conflicted. Net asset value seemed logical. It showed what the company would be worth after its debts were paid. But the number that resulted was pretty low. Esther pointed out that Electrifying was a growing company with a strong reputation, good profits, and some very clever ideas for the future. It also had great people. None of this shows up on a balance sheet, she said, but anyone buying the business would (or at least should) pay extra for all this.

A multiple of sales, she said, was a better way. Using a multiple of reported profits did not seem like a good idea. After all, Electrifying tried to manage its earnings to limit reportable profits for tax reasons, and it was bonusing out a fair amount of profits anyway. Sales growth was a simple way to capture the company's success in penetrating the market and, besides, other companies were using it.

But Allison Samuels, a new board member, was worried. "The IRS requires us to come up with a reasonable valuation," she said. "We have incentive stock options, and we have to grant them at not less than fair market value to qualify, and, besides, we want to avoid any deferred compensation tax issues under Section 409A, and part of doing that requires we develop a reasonable valuation method as well. Plus we have to take a charge to earnings for the equity we grant, so we want to base that on a realistic number. I have a fiduciary responsibility here, so I think we need something better than a guess. I think we need a formal appraisal."

Board chair Peter Easy was not persuaded. "Look, Allison, we are just a small company. Appraisals cost money, and we will need to take time to, well, appraise the appraisals. Esther's formula seems like it is good enough for other people, and, besides, how can we know that some appraiser will really understand our business? Let's just do it simply."

Eventually, the company did get an investor and later was sold to another buyer. It turned out the approach the company was using was not very close to the actual value these buyers paid. The buyers brought in their own experts to assess the value of Electrifying in detail. They offered a lot more than net asset value and somewhat more than two times sales. That pleased Electrifying's owners, but they also realized they had, effectively, given the employees a better deal than they intended. The company's attorney worried that the IRS might take a look at this transaction and decide the equity awards were priced too low and recharacterize their grants in a way that required extra taxes from employees. Fortunately, the IRS never did an audit, so the issue did not come up.

Lessons

If Electrifying was buying some expensive equipment or a new building, it would do a detailed analysis of what it was buying and what it should cost. Any other approach would seem irresponsible. When it was deciding on salary levels for top officers, it paid a compensation consultant $15,000 to do an analysis. But when it came to giving away the 15% of its equity that it ultimately awarded to employees, it did it based on a back-of-the envelope calculation. The difference between the formula-based price and the price the shares was actually worth was hundreds of thousands of dollars, even after adjusting for the fact that the company buyer was willing to pay a premium.

An outside appraisal would have cost anywhere from several thousand dollars for a very basic report that would have provided a range of value to a detailed analysis for perhaps $8,000 to $15,000. The appraiser would have first "normalized" earnings, adjusting salaries and other expenses to what a presumed outside buyer might do when running the company. The appraiser would have looked at what similar companies have sold for, assessed how much value the net assets could add, and, most importantly, computed the projected free cash flow the company would have over the next few years. That is what buyers mostly want to buy—the ability of a company to generate cash that can be used to provide a return on their investment. Buyers pay multiple for projected annual cash flow, paying a lower multiple if the risks of the investment are very high (making their annual return higher), and a higher multiple if the risk is low. Typical multiples might be anywhere from three to seven times a measure of free cash flow (such as earnings before interest, taxes, depreciation, and amortization) for closely held companies. Adjustments to per share value are then made based on whether the shares have control rights and are liquid. Lacking either, the per share value might be as much as half what the per share value might be if a company simply took its total enterprise value and divided it by the number of shares. In short, the simplistic approach Electrifying used was simply wrong.

The IRS generally does not go after private company valuations in the equity award context, even though the regulations it has published provide what appear to be some pretty strict guidelines for either having an appraisal (the gold standard) or showing that the internal appraisal is reasonable and based on an analysis by one or more people with the requisite skills to do it. A future IRS might decide these awards are worth going after. But more important is that taking the path of least resistance as Electrifying did is penny wise and pound foolish given how much money is at stake. An accurate appraisal lets companies calibrate their awards effectively and has the added benefit of providing a lot more credibility to their value for employees receiving them.

The Devil Is in the Details

Takis Makridis, Equity Methods
Yan Zhao, Equity Methods

Company XYZ (a real estate investment trust) grants an award with both a market and a performance condition, a now increasingly common structure being recommended by compensation consultants. The award ties the ultimate payout to both a relative total shareholder return (TSR) target (a market condition) and a certain accounting target (a performance condition). Many companies approach the valuation and accounting for these types of awards as homogenous. In reality, the underlying details really matter—and significantly affect the final P&L values. How a Monte Carlo simulation model should be specified and then interacted with the performance condition depends on the fact pattern of an award.

In the case of Company XYZ, the position was taken that the market condition and performance condition should be combined. Essentially, this would involve computing a Monte Carlo value for each set of performance outcome possibilities (in this case three possibilities). Three Monte Carlo values versus one was assumed to be correct since the market condition payoffs differ across performance condition payoff states. However, this approach was ultimately deemed incorrect, because it allows for the possibility of compensation expense being $0, when, in fact, this is actually not possible.

Lessons

The correct approach is to bifurcate the two conditions and calculate a Monte Carlo-based fair value for the market portion and apply variable accounting to the performance portion. This ensures that, no matter what the ultimate outcome, expense is taken related to the market condition portion of the award. But here's the key point: this will not always be the right answer! This is only the correct answer in this case based on the award fact pattern requiring bifurcation of the two conditions.

The lesson this company learned is that small details matter when dealing with esoteric performance-based awards. We have observed, on occasion, a view that valuation and accounting strategy with regard to performance-based awards is a commodity—i.e., it's straightforward and always the same regardless of where it comes from. We disagree, and we believe such a view is dangerous and reflects poor stewardship on behalf of a company's shareholders. All too often we find small nuances in award terms being missed and incorrectly treated, and ultimately jeopardizing the accuracy of the financial statements.

Statistics, Schmatistics

David Outlaw, Equity Methods

Company ABC has a unique history of granting practices, which poses implications to the correct valuation strategy for its employee stock option grants. Based on its fact pattern, a rather non-standard approach is required. Some relevant circumstances include:

- The five highest-ranking non-executive officers (NEOs) have received different awards than the rest of the company and tend to hold their options near full term, regardless of vesting schedule.
- Although the company has been public for many years, it only had a handful of irregular option grants to non-NEOs before 2008. Additionally, these pre-2008 grants had significantly different vesting than those in 2008 and later.

The rather dramatic and unfortunate situation Company ABC found itself in was that while the firm intuitively understood these facts, it was not rigorously building a valuation strategy around them. It was using simplified and homogenous assumptions for estimating expected term. Eventually, the kettle blew, with the auditors putting their feet down and insisting that a more rigorous approach was necessary.

The solution entailed building separate expected term assumptions for the two groups (NEOs and non-NEOs), whereby historical data of each group was analyzed independently of the other. Different data exclusions were required for the different groups. In fact, different expected term calculation models (yes, there's not one single model/method for calculating expected term) were also required. For example, the commonly used "midpoint method" was appropriate for the non-NEOs but entirely inappropriate for the NEO group whose exercise patterns were much more lumpy and skewed toward the award contractual term.

Lessons

When it comes to employee stock option valuation, unrefined expected term (or forfeiture rate or volatility) estimation approaches can exist for years without being scrutinized. But this is hardly a best practice and is simply asking for trouble with the external auditors. Especially as external auditors continue to gain expertise around employee stock option valuation, it is critical for companies to implement data-driven and statistically robust techniques for estimating sensitive model assumptions.

Chapter 8

Corporate Transactions

Every company begins with a dream of being successful. Whether success includes an IPO, a merger, an acquisition, or simply making more money than you spend, how your equity compensation program is managed will have an impact on that dream. Even though each of these stories could have been included in an earlier chapter, I saved them for last because they paint poignant pictures of how easy it is to lose your bottom line because someone failed to pay attention to the equity compensation program.

Change in Control or Loss of Control?

Jim Sillery, Buck Consultants

Managing equity compensation programs in a large company can be challenging and at times very stressful for human resources professionals. There are multiple constituencies to please—shareholders, investors, advisors, executives, and employees. Outsiders, like the media, need to be pleased as well. Equity plans can be highly complex, with considerations going beyond tax, accounting, and dilution concerns to issues ranging from paying for performance to creating an ownership culture.

So when that rare moment comes when everything falls into place, it is truly to be enjoyed. Such was the case in XYZ Co. The company had replaced its stock option program with performance shares several years before. Since that time, dilution had come down, making shareholders happy. Performance had been good, resulting in potential participant share distributions that were above target. Best of all, the awards had been pushed deep into the organization, and the effect of these grants on an ownership culture were becoming evident. Employee security concerns regarding consolidation in the industry had been addressed by adding change-in-control protection to all grants.

Finally, all plan documents and agreements had gone through a rigorous legal review by outside counsel to ensure that everything was in compliance with Internal Revenue Code (Code) Section 162(m) and particularly with Code Section 409A. Changes were made, documents were updated, and the plans were rolled out. Now the company was a few years into the cycle and everything was running smoothly. It had not been easy, but it was done. Everyone was happy. Life was good.

That is, until the company announced a merger. Well, really an acquisition. XYZ had an opportunity to join forces with the slightly smaller ABC Co. This was an acquisition of strategic importance since ABC's services filled a hole in XYZ's product offerings. The whole would be greater than the sum of the two parts. Better yet, ABC was a well-run company, so integration would be easy.

The deal was announced, hands were shaken ... then the dark clouds rolled in.

In the past, XYZ Co. had used several definitions of change in control in its grant agreements and plan documents. A common trigger to all was the acquisition by any individual, entity, or group of a threshold percentage of 50% or more of beneficial ownership of the combined voting power of the then-outstanding voting stock of the company. When these agreements had been reviewed by outside counsel, the definitions had all been changed to mirror the definition of change in control under Code Section 409A to ensure compliance. This meant that the threshold trigger had been changed from "50% or more" to "30% or more" with just a single trigger. (Often change in control provisions have a second trigger that is based on the award recipient's termination of employment or material change in status as a direct result of the change in control, but this one did not.)

A newly hired compensation analyst noticed this single trigger and wondered aloud. Since the deal put about 35% of the company stock into the hands of ABC shareholders, wasn't this a change in control? If so, this could mean that every unvested grant was going to accelerate at the deal. This deal? Even though the management team would remain in charge? Even though the majority of the existing board would remain in place? Additionally, couldn't this event serve as the first trigger for every executive agreement with change in control protection?

Outside counsel was called. Its legal opinion was that this deal would fall under the definition of a "group" under XYZ's change in control definition since the deal had to be approved by a majority of the shareholders rather than being transacted on an individual basis, i.e., it was being completed in a single transaction based on a group decision.

Surely, this was a defect or oversight. The compensation committee had the authority to correct defects or oversights, didn't it? This should be easy to fix.

Outside counsel was called again. Its legal opinion was that the language went beyond a defect or oversight. The language was too purposeful and too specific to argue omission. The grants would accelerate. The impact of these grants on retention, motivation, and an ownership culture would be wiped out with the transaction.

The only solution was a pre-transaction exchange for new awards that integrated amended change in control language. An exchange that had to be completed in a narrow window before shareholders voted on the transaction. An exchange that required a generous premium to employees. An exchange that would increase expense and dilution. An exchange that made many people unhappy. An exchange that made life very unpleasant for many other people.

In the end, the exchange was completed on time, the deal was done, and the markets were happy. But that rare moment had passed. It may be darkest before the dawn, but sometimes it is dawn before it gets darker.

Lessons

When designing or modifying an equity compensation plan, get the right people involved. It will not save money to get less experienced advisors who use template plans as one-size-fits-all solutions; in fact, it is likely to cost more, because you will pay them hundreds of dollars an hour to brush up on equity compensation issues if you have even minor questions about what they've recommended. Worse, these plans can cause problems that ultimately cost a lot more money to fix than hiring a true expert to design one for you in the first place would have.

Additional takeaways:

- Just because your plan is in compliance with regulations doesn't mean that the result is a good fit for your corporate goals.
- Before altering existing documents to bring them into compliance with changed regulations, analyze the proposed changes to ensure that they meet existing corporate goals and that the resulting effect on corporate goals is fully understood before the changes are made.
- When negotiating corporate transactions, i.e., mergers and acquisitions, be sure to review outstanding equity compensation plans during the diligence phase, including an analysis of how the contemplated transaction will affect the plans, so that no surprises are discovered after the deal has been finalized.
- You do not have to be an "expert" to have good insight.

Just When Did That Change in Control Happen?

Corey Rosen, National Center for Employee Ownership

One of the more frequent sources of confusion (and occasional lawsuits) is over plan documents saying that employees can exercise their equity awards "upon a change of control." If there is any ambiguity about just what this means, there can be trouble. What if there is a written agreement for a change in control, but the actual sale will not take place until regulatory approval is obtained (as happened in *Bohan v. Honeywell International,* 366 F.3d 606 [8th Cir. 2004])? What if the employee has left the company, the plan provides for acceleration of vesting on a change in control, and a merger is agreed to? Does the former employee's vesting accelerate even if she is not actually on the payroll? That was the issue in *Sanchez v. Verio, Inc.,* No. 01-11341 (5th Cir. Dec. 27, 2004).

Lessons

It's obvious that the plan needs to be explicit on these issues, as well as such matters as what happens if a subsidiary is spun off or an employee becomes a contractor rather than a W-2 employee. The problem is that the obvious can be easy to overlook in drafting a plan. No matter how much you like your plan attorney, it is a good idea to obtain one or more sample plan documents and grant agreements to cross-check whether your plan has all the relevant features you want.

Merger Soup

Jennifer George, Orrick, Herrington & Sutcliffe LLP

Over the years, I've helped a lot of large U.S. multinationals through the acquisition/ post-acquisition integration process with respect to assuming outstanding stock options and other awards granted by the target company. I actually enjoy this work more than other types of global equity support, as each deal is different, and if you dig enough, you'll find something that you have not encountered before. It's kind of like a soup that you can't see to the bottom of and only really find what's in it as you eat it.

Ideally, outside legal counsel is engaged in the due diligence process pre-close to determine if there are any significant tax or legal issues with the outstanding grants. However, for many sizable deals, companies tend to assume that any issues with global equity awards are not likely to be material to the deal, and that isn't always the case. I've been involved in pre-close due diligence work, but, more commonly, I am not brought in until after close to figure out what the damage is and help with any legal or tax filings and other issues resulting from the merger.

Merger No. 1. I remember working with one large U.S. multinational to scope out the target company (TarCo) prior to the merger being finalized, and I compiled my list of questions that I wanted TarCo to respond to with respect to equity grants that had been made outside the U.S. On the top of my list was for TarCo to confirm which countries' employer tax withholding and reporting had been done with respect to stock options that it had granted. The response came back that TarCo is a U.S. company and the plan is offered by TarCo. OK, guess that answers that. I moved to getting the option exercise details and computing the potential exposure.

Once post-close, TarCo told me that outside the U.S. it had granted stock options and restricted stock units. After asking for the details of the outstanding grants, I received spreadsheets with grants labeled "RS." The awards were really restricted stock, which sometimes does not result in the best tax treatment outside the U.S., and horrible things happen in the U.K. upon adjustment and conversion of restricted stock!

Merger No. 2. A fun discovery in connection with another merger was uncovering a program that looked like it was fine to offer in the U.S., and the target company (TarCo2) confirmed that the plan was only offered in the U.S. Looking into the thick merger soup, it came to surface that this program was also offered in Canada and Mexico, and the diligence to offer in these countries was a little less than stellar. TarCo2's in-house counsel said, "Oh, yeah, we code Canada and Mexico as part of the U.S." Needless to say, Canada and Mexico have their own securities laws and equity compensation laws.

Merger No. 3. One big U.S. multinational acquired another one (TarCo3). Come to find out, the target company's local subsidiaries in every country had adopted local severance plans pursuant to which accelerated vesting on awards would be triggered automatically after the merger if employees were terminated within a certain period of time. Although these change-in-control terms are relatively common, TarCo3 did not have equivalent terms in its domestic equity plans or award agreements. Nevertheless, once these local plans came to light, internal talk of the merger forced TarCo3 to take action to implement these favorable terms in its domestic plans on the eve of the merger.

Lessons

As demonstrated by these examples, mergers and acquisitions can be tricky business, and the information you give or receive will depend greatly upon your role in the transaction. Oftentimes the target company will give less than revelatory answers, perhaps thinking to speed up the process, but in the long run it really creates more work when the experts find a previously undisclosed mess that has to be cleaned up. In the cases above, none of these "informational failures" were deal breakers, but that can happen, too.

The important points to remember when addressing a merger or acquisition situation, depending upon your role, are:

- *Plan administrator.* Keep detailed records of all of your plans and especially any terms and conditions that are out of the ordinary.

The more organized your records, the quicker (and less expensive) the expert review will be.[1]

- *HR administrator.* Remember that if your company makes international awards you will need to ensure that local experts have been consulted regarding appropriate taxation of the company and the employee for the equity compensation. Foreign tax compliance problems can be expensive.
- *In-house counsel.* As equity compensation becomes more common in international subsidiaries, you will be responsible for knowing or consulting with local counsel to ensure that all securities laws, currency control laws, and plan qualification laws have been complied with. When plans get out of compliance, cleanup can be costly not only in legal fees but in governmental penalties.

Not-So-Plain Vanilla

Kate Forsyth, Deloitte Tax LLP

At the time of the deal everyone was so focused on getting things done they either didn't focus on the international equity or didn't figure that it was material. The international grants were not from an approved plan, so it couldn't be anything that complicated. The acquiring company agreed to honor all of the target company's equity compensation awards on a 1:1 basis, issuing a straight substitution of acquiring company stock for target company options upon exercise of the original grants. Plain vanilla.

A few months after the acquisition was completed, an individual in a foreign country who had been with the acquired company exercised a batch of stock options. The acquiring company withheld income and tax from the exercise gain. The exercising individual came back and said that the company had done something wrong—there should not be any withholding because there had never been any withholding in the past!

The acquiring company started looking into the situation, only to discover that the company it had acquired had never done any with-

1. The NCEO's *Private Company Equity Administration Handbook* (scheduled for publication in 2011) includes a CD with useful documents such as plan review samples and a corporate activity checklist.

holding or reporting for any equity ... for the entire history of the plan. Due to the fact that the local law typically treats any tax unrecovered from the employee within a certain window of time as additional taxable compensation, the tax effect of this issue for just a handful of people was well over $1 million. Given the structure of the deal, the target company's compliance failure was now a liability of the acquiring company.

Lessons

Moral of the story—there are a lot of considerations that should be reviewed upon an acquisition or merger, one of which is reviewing the history of compliance. Probably one of the most important questions that you can ask before completion of the deal is whether the acquired company correctly addressed its withholding and reporting obligations for equity compensation in the past.

Look Before You Jump!

Jon F. Doyle, International Law Partners, LLP

A number of years ago, we were retained by a large multinational company that had recently acquired another corporation with worldwide operations, including operations in France, to advise on its global equity compensation programs. In the course of M&A due diligence, the client had been told by the acquired company that it maintained a French sub plan for stock option grants in France. The sub plan was intended to provide favorable tax treatment to employees as well as the company. The acquired company had operated the stock option plan in France for a number of years as if there had been a valid sub plan. Specifically, the taxable event was intended to be the sale of acquired shares (as opposed to exercise of options). In addition, the sub plan was intended to provide that no social taxes would be payable by the employer.

Unfortunately, the acquired company had not maintained a valid sub plan. As a result, the acquired company had not paid the employer social tax (which was approximately 45% of the spread) on option exercises, and the employees reported and paid tax upon the sale of shares (as opposed to the exercise of the options). As a result, the client had assumed unpaid employer social taxes in the millions of dollars.

Lessons

The moral of the story is to perform proper M&A due diligence on global stock plans to ensure compliance with tax and other regulatory requirements, including confirmation that sub plans are valid.

Never Say Never

Fred Whittlesey, Hay Group

DEF Co. was a public company with the usual spinoff subsidiary unit. From the beginning, the company stated that the subsidiary unit would never, ever be sold or taken public. To reinforce that message, the subsidiary's equity compensation awards were structured using a phantom stock program instead of real equity. But then, way down in the details, the plan happened to include a provision that if there ever was such a transaction, the formulaic value of the phantom shares would be adjusted up to equivalent actual fair market value. Why such a provision would be included in a plan when the company was adamant that such a situation would never occur was a mystery to all concerned—and a financial disaster after all was said and done.

As the company's situation changed and the subsidiary needed external capital to remain competitive in its industry, an initial public offering emerged as the preferred solution, until someone noticed that marking up the phantom shares would wipe out the retained earnings of the company at the moment the offering occurred, requiring an unaffordable aggregate payment to employees and making an IPO unfeasible.

In the end, the investment bankers walked away from the deal and the subsidiary was eventually sold to one of its competitors at a fraction of the price that it would have brought as a public company—a price that was governed not by the subsidiary's value but by the affordability of exiting and cashing out the phantom stock plan.

Lessons

How many times can I say, "The key is to take a step back and look at the potential consequences of the plan before the plan is put in place"? Seriously, though, there are three important lessons here:

- Make sure the equity compensation plan is a business asset, not a hindrance.
- Base final plan terms on advance consideration of a company's growth model, not just an insistence of an arbitrary intention.
- Make plan terms consistent with the company's long-term roadmap, or, stated differently, don't include terms in the plan that are contrary to the company's stated intentions.

Contributors

Bruce Brumberg, myStockOptions.com

Bruce Brumberg is the editor-in-chief and co-founder of myStock-Options.com (based in Brookline, Mass.), the premier provider of Web-based educational content, tools, and custom Web sites on stock options, ESPPs, restricted stock/RSUs, SARs, and performance shares. The Web site has received numerous awards and a patent. Human Resource Executive magazine featured myStockOptions.com as one of the 10 Best HR Products. CPA Wealth Provider magazine selected the myStockOptions.com pro membership level as one of the best new products for financial and wealth advisors. Many major financial institutions, transfer agents, companies, and stock plan service providers are licensing myStockOptions.com content for their Web sites. Bruce also launched more recently www.myNQDC.com, a new Web site devoted to nonqualified deferred compensation plans.

Bruce is past president of the Boston chapter of the National Association of Stock Plan Professionals (NASPP). He is on the NASPP Advisory Board and a contributor to the Stock Plan Advisor, the association's newsletter. He has also developed and contributed to numerous other corporate, compensation, Internet, and securities law publications, conferences, and products, ranging from the popular and dramatic "Think Twice" insider trading prevention videos (www.insidertradingvideos.com) to the Corporate Executive newsletter. The "Think Twice" videos have been compared by the *New York Times* to the classic training video classics "Reefer Madness" (anti-drug video) and "Red Asphalt" (driver training). Unrelated to legal and financial topics, Bruce and his wife are the authors of the popular travel book *Watch It Made In the U.S.A: A Visitor's Guide to the Best Factory Tours & Company Museums* (www.factorytour.com). Bruce is a graduate of the University of Michigan and the University of Virginia School of Law.

Jon F. Doyle, International Law Partners LLP

Jon advises multinational companies and financial institutions on legal issues related to doing business overseas, among them outsourcing, offshoring, joint ventures, and other means of international expansion. He also advises multinational companies on global equity compensation programs. He has extensive experience advising businesses on the tax, securities, foreign exchange, labor, data privacy, and e-commerce issues they may encounter in each country where they offer stock option, stock purchase, restricted stock, phantom stock, stock appreciation right, cash bonus, venture capital, and directed share plans to their employees, directors, and consultants.

Kate Forsyth, Deloitte Tax LLP

Kate leads Deloitte's Pacific Southwest global rewards practice. She has 13 years of international tax and benefits experience with a particular focus on the design, implementation, and operation of global compensation and benefits plans.

Kate is a regular speaker on global stock plan and rewards issues and is a current board member of the Los Angeles chapter of the National Association of Stock Plan Professionals.

Kate is an Internal Revenue Service enrolled agent and holds a bachelor of commerce and a bachelor of law from the University of Queensland in Australia.

Jennifer George, Orrick, Herrington & Sutcliffe LLP

Jennifer George is a partner in the law firm of Orrick, Herrington & Sutcliffe LLP and a member of the compensation & benefits group in the San Francisco office. For over 10 years, Jennifer has focused her practice on assisting companies with offerings of equity incentives and other benefits to employees and consultants outside the United States. Most of the companies Jennifer works with are U.S. multinational companies. Her experience ranges from assisting small private companies to Fortune 500 companies. Her work on the implementation of employee incentive plans involves tax (both employee and company perspectives) and securities laws, exchange-control regulations, labor laws, and related issues. Jennifer assists companies not only with complying with current foreign rules and regulations but also with strategizing for upcoming changes and reacting quickly to these changes. She also advises companies on how to efficiently manage global programs and make smart choices regarding grant types to minimize legal filing requirements to the extent possible.

Before joining Orrick, Jennifer was a partner in the San Francisco office of Baker & McKenzie LLP, working in its global equity services group for almost 10 years.

Jennifer is a member of the Global Equity Organization (GEO), the National Association of Stock Plan Professionals (NASPP), and the California Bar Association. She is admitted to practice law in California and was previously a Certified Public Accountant.

Achaessa James, CEP, National Center for Employee Ownership

Achaessa James, CEP, is a product manager at the National Center for Employee Ownership (NCEO), where she directs its broad-based equity compensation projects, writes on current regulatory and administrative issues, and advises NCEO members on equity compensation planning.

Achaessa has designed and delivered equity administration and corporate governance education programs to attorneys, paralegals, and accounting staff. As part of her staff functions at the NCEO, she works with companies on a preliminary basis to review legal, accounting, tax, and other issues relating to all forms of equity compensation, as well as matters concerning plan design, administrative setup, and training programs. She also maintains an active consulting practice outside the NCEO to provide longer-term administrative, audit, and corporate transaction support for private companies. She has worked in the venture capital and start-up community since 1999, supporting private stock placement transactions, IPO registrations, and administering nonpublic and microcap company equity compensation plans for companies such as Shop.com, Classmates.com, Jones Soda, and Telegent Systems.

Achaessa is a Certified Equity Professional through the CEP Institute at Santa Clara University's Leavey School of Business. Achaessa was the recipient of the 2007 Marilyn J. Perkins Claassen Memorial Scholarship and the 2010 Volunteer Excellence Award. She also is a board member of the Los Angeles chapter of the National Association of Stock Plan Professionals (NASPP).

Steve Kifer, CEP, Jefferies & Co.

Steve Kifer is vice president within the global human resources and compensation group at Jefferies & Co. in Los Angeles. He is responsible for the daily administration, reporting, and management of the equity compensation plans offered at Jefferies.

With over 10 years of experience in the securities industry, Steve began his career in equity compensation with E-Trade Financial. He focused on outsourcing administration of employee stock plans and executive services. He later joined Bank of America within the global human resources and executive compensation group as assistant vice president.

Steve holds a bachelor of science degree in management science from the University of California, San Diego. He earned his Certified Equity Professional (CEP) designation in 2006 from Santa Clara University. He is currently president of the Los Angeles chapter of the National Association of Stock Plan Professionals (NASPP). Steve is also an active member and volunteer with CEP Institute at Santa Clara University.

Kim Kovacs, OptionEase

Before cofounding OptionEase Inc., Ms. Kovacs was the founding chief financial officer of ORYXE Energy International. From 2001 to 2006, Ms. Kovacs raised over $35 million in venture capital financing for ORYXE, a leading Irvine, California-based clean-tech company serving major refineries throughout the United States.

Before ORYXE Energy, Ms. Kovacs was the CFO for RosettaNet, in Santa Ana, California. RosettaNet is a not-for-profit trade consortium representing most of the Fortune 500 global companies. RosettaNet's charter is to develop e-commerce standards for rapid, mass adoption. During her tenure at RosettaNet, Ms. Kovacs worked closely with McKinsey & Co. to create, develop, and deploy a merger with the UCC.

Ms. Kovacs has also been senior partner at Tech West Partners and has served as CFO at a number of companies, including Greenland Corporation (a public company), New Media Corporation, and CROCE's. She also held a position at Deloitte & Touche as an executive consultant.

Ms. Kovacs is an active member of the Forum for Women Entrepreneurs, an advisor to the Association of Women in Technology, and an active member of E2.

Ms. Kovacs graduated with honors from California State University at San Diego with a bachelor of science degree in business administration/finance.

Paul Leisey, Equity Methods

Paul is responsible for the efficient and accurate productization of Equity Methods' intellectual capital, which includes designing and building the automated technology processes that power end-to-end compliance solutions. Paul's area of focus involves emerging client needs and customized client solutions. Since 2010 he has been focused on driving new capabilities related to IFRS, employee stock purchase plan (ESPP) compliance, and dynamic report customization.

Since joining Equity Methods, Paul has provided critical support to the advancement and development of the professional services group. Well-versed in the theoretical underpinnings of valuation and derivatives pricing, Paul has an applied financial economics background that includes research on modeling techniques ranging from Monte Carlo simulation to fixed-income valuation methods. Paul combines his extensive theoretical background and understanding of applied economics with a deep understanding of the technicalities of ASC 718 to assist companies in their ASC 718 compliance efforts. Paul holds a BS in finance and a master's in finance (MMF), both from the Eller College of Management at the University of Arizona.

Takis Makridis, Equity Methods

Takis Makridis is the head of the Equity Methods consulting group, a Bank of America Merrill Lynch company. In his role, he oversees client delivery, operations, sales, marketing, and R&D. Takis has worked closely with finance and human resources executives to address their equity compensation accounting, valuation, and financial reporting needs and remains critically engaged with thought leaders from consulting firms, public accounting, and academia in addressing emerging issues. The Equity Methods consulting group assists over 400 companies in properly valuing and accounting for their equity compensation instruments, with a particular focus on large and generally complex programs.

Takis is a nationally recognized speaker at industry conferences across the country and frequently leads executive briefing sessions and firm Webinars to enhance knowledge sharing among client firms and disseminate best practices throughout the industry. Takis is the author of *Advanced Topics in Equity Compensation Accounting* and coauthor (with Barbara Baksa) of Accounting for Equity Compensation (third through fifth editions), both published by the National Center for Employee Ownership. Both are required texts for the Certified Equity Professional (CEP) designation. Takis is also an advisory board member of the Certified Equity Professional Institute and the Department of Finance at the W.P. Carey School of Business at Arizona State University. Takis has published articles in various technical and business publications and has also been cited in media publications such as the *New York Times* and *Compliance Week*. Takis holds a BS in economics and finance from Arizona State University and an MBA from Oxford University.

Mark Miller, Deloitte Tax LLP

Mark is a senior manager with Deloitte Tax. He leads the Northern Pacific region of the global rewards practice, specializing in global compensation and benefits consulting for internationally mobile and international "domestic" employees. Mark has over nine years of experience consulting in the field of employee equity compensation, advising multinational clients on all aspects of equity remuneration including core plan design and administration, communications strategies, investor relations, tax and regulatory compliance, and tax minimization strategies.

In his role within the global rewards practice of Deloitte Tax, Mark supports a number of high-profile Pacific Northwest and Bay Area clients in designing, implementing, and maintaining compliant and strategic equity programs for internationally mobile employee populations.

Mark has been an active speaker at various U.S. and international conferences and events for over six years. He began his career in the

United Kingdom, specializing in U.K. and global equity based remuneration and compensation planning. He has been working within the West Coast practice of Deloitte Tax for the past six years. Mark is a Certified Equity Professional (CEP) in the U.S. and a Chartered Tax Advisor (CTA, ATT) in the United Kingdom.

David Outlaw, Equity Methods

While at Equity Methods, David has specialized in working on advanced option valuation consulting engagements, including lattice valuations of option exchange programs and other complex modification valuation projects. He leverages his quantitative skills and a solid understanding of option valuation toward assisting clients in addressing the compliance requirements of ASC Topic 718, and he has managed numerous plain-vanilla option valuation engagements. He is currently a SAS certified base programmer and is working toward obtaining the advanced programmer certification. David holds a BS in finance and a BS in economics, both from the Barrett Honors College at Arizona State University. Within the W.P. Carey School of Business, he was a member of the Beta Gamma Sigma and Phi Kappa Phi honor societies.

Corey Rosen, National Center for Employee Ownership

Corey Rosen, PhD, is the co-founder and former executive director of the NCEO. He is co-author, along with John Case and Martin Staubus, of *Equity: Why Employee Ownership Is Good for Business* (Harvard Business School Press, May 2005). Over the years, he has written, edited, or contributed to dozens of books, articles, and research papers on employee ownership. He is generally regarded as the leading expert on employee ownership in the world.

Rosen received his PhD in political science from Cornell University in 1973, after which he taught politics at Ripon College in Wisconsin before being named an American Political Science Association Congressional Fellow in 1975. In 1981, he formed the NCEO. He stepped down as the NCEO's executive director in April 2011 and now serves as the senior staff member.

Robyn Shutak, National Association of Stock Plan Professionals

Robyn is the education director for the NASPP. Her responsibilities include implementing new educational programs and coordinating Webcasts on industry-related current events for the organization. Prior to joining the NASPP, Robyn was the senior manager, equity compensation, for Entropic Communications Inc., where she managed all aspects of the company's global equity programs. Robyn has also held various equity compensation related positions with several other San Diego-area publicly traded companies, such as Leap Wireless, Biosite Inc., Applied Micro Circuits Corp., and Jack in the Box Inc.

Robyn is a Certified Equity Professional (CEP). She holds a bachelor's degree in English literature from San Diego State University and a paralegal certificate from the ABA paralegal program at the University of San Diego. She was the programming director for the San Diego Chapter of the NASPP for more than seven years and has been a member of the curriculum committee of the CEP Institute for four years.

Jim Sillery, Buck Consultants

Jim Sillery is a principal in Buck Consultants' Chicago office. For nearly 30 years, he has advised companies in a broad range of industries, addressing both domestic and global compensation issues. His primary focus has been helping companies to develop total compensation solutions that provide a competitive advantage in today's rapidly changing global markets.

Prior to joining Buck, Jim provided consulting services for several consulting firms, ranging from executive compensation boutiques to large, global human capital consultancies. In corporate roles, Jim has directed the compensation, benefits, and human resources technology functions at several major global corporations.

Jim is an adjunct professor at The John Marshall Law School. He has an MBA from Keller Graduate School of Management and a bachelor of science degree in psychology from the University of Scranton. Jim has been recognized by WorldatWork with a lifetime achievement award and currently serves on the board of directors of the Chicago Compensation Association.

Mike Stevens, Alston & Bird LLP

Mike Stevens is a partner in the Atlanta office of Alston & Bird. He focuses on executive compensation matters, with a particular emphasis on tax, securities, and corporate governance issues relating to stock plans, incentive compensation arrangements, executive employment and change in control agreements, and deferred compensation. Mr. Stevens frequently advises clients with respect to executive compensation issues relating to mergers and acquisitions and other corporate transactions.

Mr. Stevens is a frequent speaker and writer on a variety of matters relating to executive compensation and securities aspects of benefit plans. He has served on the faculty of the Institute of Applied Management and Law and recently has spoken for the National Association of Stock Plan Professionals (NASPP), the National Center for Employee Ownership (NCEO), the Society of Corporate Secretaries and Governance Professionals, and the State Bar of Georgia.

Mr. Stevens received his law degree, with distinction, from Emory University School of Law in 1993, where he was an editor of the Emory Law Journal, was elected to the Order of the Coif, and received the Lexis Excellence in Writing Award. He received his undergraduate degree, with high honors, from Emory University in 1990, where he was elected to Phi Beta Kappa.

Dan Walter, Performensation Consulting

Dan Walter, CEP, is the president and CEO of Performensation Consulting. For more than 15 years, he has assisted companies with both executive and broad-based compensation programs. He provides perspectives on end-to-end solutions for private and public companies in both the United States and abroad. Dan's expertise includes equity compensation, executive programs, performance-based pay, and talent management issues. His experience with these programs includes diagnosis, design, communication, administration, and reporting. Dan has experience with all forms of equity, including stock options, restricted shares and units, stock purchase plans, and performance-based programs. Dan has been the architect of software solutions and has significant experience in the administrative and technological best practices for these programs. In addition to writing about equity compensation, Dan does dozens of presentations on the subject every year at Webinars, conferences, and other events.

Fred Whittlesey, Hay Group

Fred is a senior principal with Hay Group, based in San Francisco. He specializes in compensation strategy, director and executive compensation, and equity-based compensation with a primary focus on entrepreneurial companies in the technology, life sciences, and other growth sectors.

Fred is the co-founder and a past board member of the Global Equity Organization (GEO), a founding member of the National Association of Stock Plan Professionals (NASPP) and past president of its Orange County chapter, and past chair of the advisory board for the Certified Equity Professional Institute (CEPI). He served as a faculty member and developer for WorldatWork's "Accounting and Finance for the Human Resources Professional" certification course as well as the basic and advanced executive compensation courses, and delivered instruction both in the classroom and online.

Fred has authored dozens of articles in major compensation journals and periodicals and has presented his ideas at compensation conferences around the world. His most recent published works include "Understanding Executive Pay Equity and Fairness: Ratios and Rationality" in *WorldatWork Journal*; "How Much is 'Market' Driving Global Equity Compensation Trends ... and What Does 'Market' Mean?" in *GEOnomics 2010*; "Behavioral Economics and Equity Compensation" in *GEOnomics 2009*; and "Measuring the ROI of Compensation Expenditures" in *The Compensation Handbook*. He is the host of "Keeping Up with Fred Whittlesey," an audiocast sponsored by GEO, and is a regular contributor to The Advisors' Blog on CompensationStandards.com.

Fred received his MBA from UCLA and a BA in industrial/organizational psychology from San Diego State University. He has earned the Certified Equity Professional (CEP), Certified Executive Compensation Professional (CECP), and Certified Compensation Professional (CCP) designations.

Yan Zhao, Equity Methods

Yan's interest in quantitative finance began in the area of fixed-income valuation, with topics ranging from mortgage-backed securities to caps, floors, and swaps. While studying finance at the University of Arizona, he gained understanding of several financial models as well as derivatives pricing, with work ranging from Merton's model of credit risk to interest rate modeling methods such as the Black-Derman-Toy and Vasicek models. Prior to joining Equity Methods, Yan spent three years as a research assistant conducting research in chemistry at the University of Arizona under grants from the U.S. Department of Energy and the National Science Foundation. Yan also served as an instructor at the University of Arizona, where he trained students in problem solving and communication skills in the physical sciences. At Equity Methods, Yan uses his quantitative skills in focusing on advanced valuations that use Monte Carlo simulations, as well as more complex or sensitive valuations of plain-vanilla awards. Yan holds an MS in finance and an MA in chemistry, both from the University of Arizona.

About the NCEO

The National Center for Employee Ownership (NCEO) is widely considered to be the leading authority in employee ownership in the U.S. and the world. Established in 1981 as a nonprofit information and membership organization, it now has over 2,500 members, including companies, professionals, unions, government officials, academics, and interested individuals. It is funded entirely through the work it does.

The NCEO's mission is to provide the most objective, reliable information possible about employee ownership at the most affordable price possible. As part of the NCEO's commitment to providing objective information, it does not lobby or provide ongoing consulting services. The NCEO publishes a variety of materials on employee ownership and participation; holds dozens of seminars, Webinars, and conferences on employee ownership annually; and offers a variety of online courses. The NCEO's work includes extensive contacts with the media, both through articles written for trade and professional publications and through interviews with reporters. It has written or edited several books for outside publishers. The NCEO's Web site is www.nceo.org.

NCEO Membership Benefits

- The bimonthly newsletter *Employee Ownership Report,* which covers ESOPs, equity compensation, and employee participation.
- Access to the members-only area of the NCEO's Web site, which includes a searchable newsletter archive, a discussion forum, a database of service providers, and more.
- Substantial discounts on publications, online courses, and events produced by the NCEO.
- Free access to live Webinars on ESOPs and equity compensation.
- The right to contact the NCEO for answers to general or specific questions regarding employee ownership.

An introductory NCEO membership costs $90 for one year ($100 outside the U.S.) and covers an entire company at all locations, a single professional offering services in this field, or a single individual with a business interest in employee ownership. Full-time students and faculty members who are not employed in the business sector may join at the academic rate of $40 for one year ($50 outside the U.S.).

Selected NCEO Publications

The NCEO offers a variety of publications on all aspects of employee ownership and participation. Below are some of our publications. To obtain the most current information on what we have available, visit us on the Web at www.nceo.org or call us at 510-208-1300.

Equity Compensation Plans

- *If I'd Only Known That* is a guide to common mistakes in equity compensation and what to do about them.

  $25 for NCEO members, $35 for nonmembers

- *The Stock Options Book* is a straightforward, comprehensive overview covering the legal, accounting, regulatory, and design issues involved in implementing a stock option or stock purchase plan.

  $35 for NCEO members, $50 for nonmembers

- *Selected Issues in Equity Compensation* is more detailed and specialized than *The Stock Options Book,* with chapters on issues such as repricing, securities issues, and evergreen options.

  $35 for NCEO members, $50 for nonmembers

- *Accounting for Equity Compensation* is a guide to the accounting rules that govern equity compensation programs in the U.S.

  $35 for NCEO members, $50 for nonmembers

- *The Decision-Maker's Guide to Equity Compensation* describes the various types of equity compensation, how they work, and how to decide how much to give and to whom.

  $35 for NCEO members, $50 for nonmembers

- *Beyond Stock Options* is a complete guide, including annotated model plans, to phantom stock, restricted stock, stock appreciation rights, performance awards, and more. Includes a CD with plan documents.

  $35 for NCEO members, $50 for nonmembers

Employee Stock Ownership Plans (ESOPs)

- *Understanding ESOPs* is an overview of the issues involved in establishing and operating an ESOP.

  $25 for NCEO members, $35 for nonmembers

- *ESOPs and Corporate Governance* covers everything from shareholder rights to the impact of Sarbanes-Oxley to choosing a fiduciary.

  $25 for NCEO members, $35 for nonmembers

- *The ESOP Company Board Handbook* is a guide for board members in ESOP companies.

  $25 for NCEO members, $35 for nonmembers

- *Executive Compensation in ESOP Companies* discusses executive compensation issues, special ESOP considerations, and a survey of executive compensation in ESOP companies.

  $25 for NCEO members, $35 for nonmembers

- *S Corporation ESOPs* introduces the reader to how ESOPs work and then discusses the legal, valuation, administrative, and other issues associated with S corporation ESOPs.

  $25 for NCEO members, $35 for nonmembers

- *Don't Do That* is a guide to common mistakes in operating an ESOP and what to do about them.

  $25 for NCEO members, $35 for nonmembers

To join the NCEO as a member or to order publications, use the order form on the following page, order online at www.nceo.org, or call us at 510-208-1300. If you join at the same time you order publications, you will receive the members-only publication discounts.

Order Form

This book is published by the National Center for Employee Ownership (NCEO). You can order additional copies online at our Web site, www.nceo.org; by telephoning the NCEO at 510-208-1300; by faxing this page to the NCEO at 510-272-9510; or by sending this page to the NCEO at 1736 Franklin Street, 8th Floor, Oakland, CA 94612. If you join as an NCEO member with this order, or are already an NCEO member, you will pay the discounted member price for any publications you order.

Name

Organization

Address

City, State, Zip (Country)

Telephone Fax Email

Method of Payment: ❑ Check (payable to "NCEO") ❑ Visa ❑ M/C ❑ AMEX

Credit Card Number

Signature Exp. Date

Checks are accepted only for orders from the U.S. and must be in U.S. currency.

Title	Qty.	Price	Total

Tax: California residents add 9.75% sales tax (on publications only, not membership)

Shipping: In the U.S., first publication $5, each add'l $1; elsewhere, we charge exact shipping costs to your credit card, plus a $10 handling surcharge; no shipping charges for membership

Introductory NCEO Membership: $90 for one year ($100 outside the U.S.)

Subtotal	$
Sales Tax	$
Shipping	$
Membership	$
TOTAL DUE	$